SURROUNDED BY Angels

A CEO's Journey of Faith in the War Against Prostate Cancer

THEODORE MISTRA

SURROUNDED BY ANGELS
Copyright ©2023 Theodore Mistra

Published by Castle Quay Books
An imprint of Castle Quay Communications Inc.
Burlington, Ontario, Canada and Jupiter, Florida, U.S.A.
416-573-3249 | info@castlequaybooks.com | www.castlequaybooks.com

Edited by Marina Hofman Willard
Cover design and book interior by Burst Impressions

All rights reserved. This book or parts thereof may not be reproduced in any form without prior written permission of the publishers.

Unless otherwise marked, Scripture quotations are taken from the New King James Version. Copyright © 1979, 1980, 1982. Thomas Nelson Inc., Publishers. Used by permission. All rights reserved worldwide. • Scripture marked (NIV) are taken from the Holy Bible, New International Version®, NIV® Copyright ©1973, 1978, 1984, 2011 by Biblica, Inc.® Used by permission. All rights reserved worldwide.

978-1-988928-76-0 Soft Cover
978-1-988928-77-7 E-book

Library and Archives Canada Cataloguing in Publication

Title: Surrounded by angels : a CEO's journey of faith in the war against prostate cancer / Theodore Mistra.
Names: Mistra, Theodore, author.
Identifiers: Canadiana 20220491321 | ISBN 9781988928760 (softcover)
Subjects: LCSH: Mistra, Theodore. | LCSH: Prostate—Cancer—Patients—United States—Biography. | LCSH:
       Prostate—Cancer—Patients—Religious life—United States. | LCSH: Prostate—Cancer—Treatment. |
   LCSH: Christian biography—United States. | LCGFT: Autobiographies.
Classification: LCC RC280.P7 M57 2023 | DDC 362.19699/4630092—dc23

AUTHOR'S NOTE

This book was written to glorify God, to keep the focus on how the Lord can work in our lives, and not on the specifics of any one type of preferred medical treatment. To protect the privacy of the many friends and medical personnel who played key roles in the story, most of the names have been altered. The real names are noted as such.

Although the writer's name given here is a pen name, the author is available to personally share his experience with those who seek encouragement in their own battle with prostate cancer. Contact the publisher if you wish to speak with the author.

CONTENTS

PROLOGUE	7
1. MY JOURNEY BEGINS	11
2. GOD'S PEACE	17
3. I WILL FOLLOW	25
4. THE SPIRIT WITHIN	29
5. A MESSAGE FROM GOD	33
6. TENDING MY FLOCK	37
7. IN GOD'S HANDS	41
8. THE ARMOR OF GOD	47
9. WHERE GOD LEADS	53
10. ON EAGLE'S WINGS	59
11. SERVING OTHERS	65
12. THE LIGHT OF CHRIST	71
13. MINISTERING ANGELS	77
14. THE NEXT STEP OF FAITH	79
15. BEYOND FEAR	81
16. BY GOD'S GRACE	87
17. CROSSED PATHS	91
18. THIS JOURNEY ENDS	95
19. THE NEW THING	99
20. WHEN I CALL	103
RESOURCES	107

PROLOGUE

The LORD is for me among those who help me.
Psalm 118:7

It was fifteen years ago, on October 23, that I learned that I had cancer. After a momentary flash of fear, I realized that I had an important choice to make: I could live in fear, or I could live by faith.

As a follower of Jesus Christ, I determined right then that I wanted to face this battle boldly, not timidly; calmly, not with apprehension. I decided to place my trust in God to help me face this huge new challenge with courage, wisdom, joy, and calm. To my eternal thankfulness, God filled me with an amazing sense of peace.

God had helped me through tough times before. I am a senior executive for a life sciences company located in the Midwest. Like any business, our company has suffered through its trials and tribulations. We've lost major clients, experienced economic slowdowns, computer meltdowns and staff turnover, and endured other crises along the way. Despite the setbacks, though, our company has continued to grow. As a man of faith, I had always believed that God had been there for me corporately. Perhaps His faithfulness to me in company matters helped me believe that now He would be there for me personally as well—through my personal trial with cancer.

When it came to my health, I had always been a bit compulsive. I'd never truly "let go and let God" be in control; I guess I always had felt I knew best and could stay a step or two ahead of Him. Besides, He was busy with bigger things, right? But now, knowing that I had cancer, I realized that nearly every success I had ever experienced in my life had come only after I had asked God for direction. I needed to do the same now. I resolved that, this time, I was not going to get out in front of God. This time I was going to pray for guidance and let God lead me.

As I wrote in my journal:

There is only one thing He wants, only unconditional and complete surrender, trusting in our Father in heaven. Once we truly see God at work, we will never be concerned again about things that happen.

> God led me to trust Him about being a father, and I surrendered to Him. God showed me His glory. Peace. God led me to trust Him about my company. I surrendered to Him, and He gave me peace. Now God wants me to surrender my body and my anxiety about my health, which has always been something I thought I could control. Despite my careful attention to my health, I never truly trusted God about this. God is now bringing me deeper to trust Him always in all things.

With this health problem, I knew my life would change dramatically in the months ahead. But I did not fear what those months might bring, nor did I fear the outcome of my battle with cancer. Such peace and strength can be only from God. He held me up and sustained me during those difficult months, and I sensed His presence every day—especially through the supportive people He surrounded me with every step along the way. I consider those wonderful people my "angels."

I find myself so thankful to God, not only for His mercies, but for allowing me to go through this experience and to share it with others. My hope and prayer is that my story will be of encouragement to you or to someone you care deeply about—someone who may be traveling a journey similar to my own. This book is my testimony, my journey of faith, and how God walked with me in my war against cancer and taught me things I would never have learned otherwise.

Many years ago I was introduced to the Reginald B. Cherry Ministries[1] of Houston, Texas. Dr. Cherry was a successful medical doctor who sensed the Lord's leading to write and teach about the relationship between faith and health.

One of his books is *God's Pathway to Healing Prostate*. Several years before my diagnosis, I had purchased this book because I knew prostate cancer is one of the most widespread cancers affecting men, and was curious about what God had put on Dr. Cherry's heart. While I had no premonition that it would affect me, I always believed in being prepared—especially for any health circumstances. Little did I know that I was arming myself for my own battle; I simply thought Cherry's book would be a good resource that I could share with other men, not as a launching pad for my own fight.

---

[1] Actual name.

God made us unique creatures in His image. We each are special and different, yet all of us are part of God's family. Once we recognize the sanctity of our relationship with God, it also becomes evident that God has a special plan for each of us. Just as He gives us different gifts for His glory, He also gives us different pathways through life. When I was told I had cancer and resolved to face the challenge with faith instead of fear, I felt a deep inner assurance that God had a plan, a pathway for me to follow in my journey toward healing.

I recalled Reginald Cherry's book, found it on my bookshelf, and reopened its pages. Dr. Cherry's words jumped from those pages into my heart.

Each of us has our own unique pathway to healing, Cherry asserts, and we must immerse ourselves in prayer and let God's Holy Spirit lead us along that path. All too often we rush, panic, and get ahead of the Spirit because we want to right the situation in our own way, in our own timing. But, tough as it is, trusting God means letting go and letting Him guide us. This doesn't mean becoming resigned and passive in our treatment; on the contrary, it means gearing up for action but basing our action on intensive prayer for God to lead us to the right people, the right protocols, and to *"make our path straight"* (Proverbs 3:6 NIV).

As soon I as received the startling news of my condition, I prayed almost unceasingly for guidance. My wife, Martha, also started to pray. Close friends started to pray. I began making phone calls, seeking advice and direction. It seemed that God brought to mind several key people to call—people who knew people who could help me. One call led to another.

Within forty-eight hours from my diagnosis, I had a clear pathway mapped out—a course of action that I knew in my heart was from God. I felt the deep peace that He promises in Philippians 4:7, *a peace that surpasses all human understanding*. The burden lifted from my shoulders.

No, the journey wasn't easy. Battling cancer never is. But we can either shrink back in fear or step forward in faith. With God's Son, Jesus Christ, in my life, fear was not an option for me. I chose faith, and that made the tough journey easier, but also more meaningful.

Let me share with you what I mean …

1.
MY JOURNEY BEGINS

*We know that all things work together for good to those who love
God, to those who are called according to His purpose.*

Romans 8:28

October 17, I had a biopsy of my prostate. Three days later, I still did not know the results of my biopsy. Knowing that waiting and fretting over the results would not have done me any good, I decided to set aside my concerns and enjoy some time with my children. It was a wonderful weekend in which I was able to devote full time and attention, making certain we all enjoyed ourselves.

The following Monday I still did not hear from the doctor. By then I was feeling somewhat anxious—not oppressively so, but a bit nervous. I recall that during a meeting my cell phone rang, and for a moment I experienced a twang of fear. But the phone call was not from the doctor, and Monday evening I was still waiting for him to call me with my test results.

On Tuesday morning I still had not received a call, so I decided to pay the doctor a visit.

"I know the results are complete," I said to his receptionist. "I would like a copy of my report, please."

"Please wait," she said as she vanished down the hall. After several minutes she reappeared and announced, "The doctor wants to talk to you."

I walked to the examining room, and within a few moments, the doctor appeared and said, "None of us here thought you had cancer, but you do. Here's the report."

Then he handed me a DVD. "I don't have time to speak with you," he said. "Go home and look at the DVD. It will answer all of your questions. Then call my receptionist and make a thirty-minute appointment."

To deliver such stunning news so abruptly seemed both insensitive and unprofessional. Granted, I had walked in without an appointment, but I had cancer. This doctor knew it and should have called me when he initially received the results. Instead, he had forced me to wait two days while the report sat on his desk; he might have procrastinated longer had I not walked in and asked for the results.

I was more alarmed than angry. If this had happened to me, how many other people did it happen to? Being busy is no excuse: doctors have a responsibility to serve their patients in a compassionate and timely manner. This is integral to the Hippocratic Oath.

I left his office and never went back.

Thankfully, such callousness on the part of caregivers never happened again during my journey. It was a single negative incident that was more than superseded by the many positive experiences: other medical professionals made gentleness and kindness a part of their everyday protocol with me.

As I left the doctor's office that day, it was not with fear: the biggest thing on my heart was a distinct feeling that God wanted to use this major challenge in my life so that I could, in turn, help others in their own fights against cancer.

"If that's Your desire for me, Lord, then use this to teach me what You want me to learn," I prayed. "Give me strength for my battle, and show me how I can encourage and help others"

I called Martha, who was on her way to church. She is a member of a prayer team, caring men and women who meet regularly to pray for those who are ill. Martha and I are both supporters of this ministry. After I told her the news, she asked, "Would you like to come and have the folks pray for you?" I agreed and met her at the church.

"I am not fearful," I told the group. In my heart, God was impressing upon me that I was to help others through the trial which now lay ahead of me, but I did not say this to the others.

"Will you pray for me?" I asked instead.

"We already have," one of them replied. "Before you got here. And God spoke to us. Want to know what He said?"

How could I turn that down? "You bet!" I answered.

"Okay, Ted. As we prayed, we all sensed God telling us that you are to be His servant. He has chosen you for this, and He will use your journey for good."

This was confirming what God had already placed on my heart. I had not spoken of this to anyone—not even Martha. Nevertheless, God gave these people the same message He had given to me only a few minutes before.

As group members gathered around me and placed their hands on me for prayer, they spoke additional words of encouragement to me—words straight from the Scriptures.

One shared, *"'As the new heavens and the new earth which I will make shall remain before Me,'" says the* Lord, *"'so shall your descendants and your name remain'"* (Isaiah 66:22).

Another member quoted Isaiah 65:17: *"Behold, I create new heavens and a new earth; and the former shall not be remembered or come to mind."*

And from another: *"We, according to His promise, look for new heavens and a new earth in which righteousness dwells"* (2 Peter 3:13).

One member of the group asserted, "Ted, I want to bring you closer to God."

I'm already close to God, I thought. *How can I get closer to Him than I already feel?*

"Ted, God is going to use this trial to go deeper into the recesses of your heart and to purify you further. This will all be to God's glory. May I pray for you and anoint you with oil?" Anointing with oil is a biblical practice still used today by many Christians as they pray for healing.

"Of course," I agreed.

Together we prayed again, not only for my healing, but that God would indeed draw me closer to Him throughout my journey—that He would refine me and enable me to minister comfort to others from an empathic heart. As we wrapped up our prayer time, another passage from Isaiah was shared with me:

You whom I have taken from the ends of the earth,
And called from its farthest regions,
And said to you,
"You are My servant,
I have chosen you and have not cast you away:
Fear not, for I am with you;
Be not dismayed, for I am your God.
I will strengthen you,
Yes, I will help you,
I will uphold you with My righteous right hand." (Isaiah 41:9–10)

I would draw on that verse many times in the coming weeks. I wholeheartedly recommend that every reader, no matter what challenge you may be facing, commit at least verse 10 of this wonderful passage to memory and call upon it often. You will be blessed, just as I was every time I reviewed the passage's promise. It was my reassurance that I was not in this battle alone, that God would strengthen, help, and uphold me with His righteous right hand.

And it's His promise to you as well. You can bank on it.

After this beautiful time of prayer with the prayer team, I returned to my office and felt the presence of the Holy Spirit begin to lead me to action.

I picked up the telephone and began calling. The first call was to a dear friend who had undergone prostate treatment two years earlier and was considered cured. Jack was a tremendous source of encouragement. He suggested I call his doctor at the Mayo

Clinic, Dr. Samuel Peterson, one of the top prostate cancer surgeons in the nation. "Use my name as a referral," Jack said.

I then called another friend, Michael, a retired doctor who had trained at the Mayo Clinic. Interestingly, Michael also recommended Dr. Peterson and said he would refer me.

My next call was to Dr. Peterson's secretary. What an unexpected blessing she was! Dr. Peterson's secretary was friendly, attentive, and compassionate. Yes, I had been a Mayo patient for many years for routine physicals, but never for cancer. She didn't know me. No matter. She asked me a few questions about my overall health and the results of my biopsy, then promised to get back to me.

True to her word, Dr. Peterson's secretary called back and asked if I would like an appointment. Between calls, Martha and I had prayed unceasingly, and given my biopsy and my age (59), we had come to the conclusion that surgery was most likely my best option. So I was ready for the call! Within forty-eight hours of my diagnosis, I had an appointment and a surgery date with one of the world's foremost prostate surgeons—and I was not even his patient yet.

After the rocky start with my original doctor and the meaningful prayer time with new friends, God was ministering to me through "angels" who brought me compassion and encouragement. He was preparing the way. I knew in my heart that we were already on the path toward healing.

I had not been feeling well for some time. Several months prior to my diagnosis, I had realized I was feeling different. I had felt drained, exhausted.

Why am I so tired? This is ridiculous. This just wasn't me, I thought, and decided to investigate further.

The doctor told me to relax, that nothing was wrong. Yet I could not relax. The stamina I was so accustomed to just wasn't there. It was this seemingly sudden drain of energy that God used to capture my attention.

Remember my ongoing anxiety about health I mentioned earlier? Well, this time it served me well. Even though I had taken a full battery of tests just six months before, I decided to repeat them.

Thank God I did. Within three months my PSA results had crossed the threshold (from 4.0 to 4.8), enough to cause concern. I insisted on a biopsy. This would be my second biopsy in five years, yet I felt compelled to demand it.

At the time, I was reading *Mover of Men and Mountains* by R.G. LeTourneau.[2] In that book the author wrote a wonderful testimony about faith at work, at home, and in the community.

Robert Gilmore LeTourneau was a godly man who glorified God for empowering him to do His work. He said, "When God has a job for us to do, He will give us the strength and the ability to do it."

God had a job for me to do. He wanted me to give my testimony about my health so that others would be encouraged. God gave me the strength that transcends all human understanding. My cancer was not about me; it was about God and His message and promises.

---

2 Actual name.

2.
GOD'S PEACE

*Peace I leave with you, My peace I give to you; not as the world
gives do I give to you. Let not your heart be troubled,
neither let it be afraid.*

John 14:27

Jane Baker, M.D., was a professor at a Midwestern university medical center. She was also deeply involved in their integrative medicine program. Jane is a spiritual person, and has been a good friend of ours for many years.

Jane's children knew my children growing up. They went to school together. Jane and Martha attended a moms' prayer group together. I knew her personally long before I ever knew her professionally, when I volunteered at the medical center.

The day I learned that I had cancer, in addition to making phone calls, I also had emailed Dr. Jane Baker inquiring about alternative treatments.

It didn't take long for her to call me back.

"I'm at the airport in Washington, D.C.," she told me over her cell phone. "I've got some time before my flight back home." She went on to tell me that she had just attended a seminar at the National Institutes of Health (NIH) and the National Cancer Institute on alternative treatments for cancer. One session had addressed potential alternative-medicine treatments for prostate cancer.

"Ted, we're finding that high doses of particular vitamins, administered intravenously, will selectively kill cancer cells while leaving healthy cells undamaged," she said. "I'm confident these infusions could be effective for you as well."

Upon her return, Dr. Baker discussed my care with the doctors at the National Institutes of Health. Because there was not yet enough reliable evidence to support the vitamin infusion theory, she was concerned that the Mayo Clinic would reject the protocol that she wanted to start me on right away. One of the doctors in the urology surgery residency at Mayo Clinic did express some concern about the treatments; however, after reading some articles published on the subject, he soon supported her decision. I soon became the beneficiary of Dr. Baker's sweet inspiration.

Dr. Baker and one of the researchers at the NIH discussed my case further, and they both believed that the vitamin infusions might very well destroy my cancer cells, possibly postponing—or even decreasing—the need to remove my prostate.

I was humbled at how God had been working in my life; how it appeared that He had been planning for my treatment all along. Two years before, I had volunteered at the medical center because I wanted to help. I never imagined at that time that I would be a patient of Dr. Baker's. Because I had determined to trust God and move forward in faith, not fear, I cannot believe it was a coincidence that Jane Baker attended a seminar on alternative treatments for cancer at the same time I learned I had prostate cancer. Nor do I believe it was coincidence that God had put on my heart to send her an email message inquiring about alternative treatments. Dr. Baker and I instantly knew that God had been orchestrating all of this from the beginning.

I also believed that God had inspired Dr. Baker to use His creation—natural nutrients—to heal diseases. God did not give Dr. Baker her gift in order to compete with the gifts He had given the other doctors. I am convinced that God gave each of them their own unique gifts so they could all work together, complementing one another's training and strengths, serving one another for the healing of all of God's children.

David Wilkerson,[3] the founding pastor of the Times Square Church in New York City, publishes a monthly newsletter for his contributors. The message in a recent issue, "Winning Our Private War," summarized and confirmed the personal calling that God had placed on my heart. As soldiers in God's army, Wilkerson suggested, our own private wars are how God strengthens and teaches us wisdom.

"When we are at the center of our conflicts," he wrote, "those close to us depend on our example. God needs us to fight our battles wholeheartedly, relying on His help and strength, because if He were to pull us out those around us may suffer and fall away: You are the one who God uses to drive out the enemy. You are the one He wants to teach how to war. You are the warrior who God works through. And He is using your example to strengthen weaker brethren."

---

[3] Actual name.

The calling that God had placed on my heart was not an easy one. He wanted me to go through this battle with cancer so that He could work through me to strengthen, help, and uphold others who also are facing such a battle. I didn't want to let Him down in this. I prayed that the Lord would strengthen and uphold me so that my example to others would bless them and glorify Him.

A close friend of mine had been preoccupied with something lately. But he hadn't offered to tell me what he was going through. I decided to let him know I had prostate cancer. After I shared my news with him, he opened up to me. To my surprise, he told me that he had prostate cancer too.

"I just completed my therapy today," he said, "and I'm fine. You're going to be fine, too." We studied each other for a long moment.

"This is not a coincidence," he mused.

My friend was right. His hearing that I had prostate cancer on the same day that he had completed his therapy for prostate cancer was not a coincidence.

"I believe God helped me so I could help you," he asserted. "Now you're going to be able to help somebody after you go through your battle."

The summer before I found out I had cancer, God had put on my heart a promise: I would be more fruitful in my next twenty years than I had been in my earlier years. I had shared this conviction with a good friend of mine. "I cannot even begin to think about retirement yet," I'd told him.

In hindsight, God had already promised me that I would be well, that He would not take away His promise. This trial was just a temporary obstacle that could be overcome.

In the days following my diagnosis, I pondered God's promise. I reasoned that God did not give me my cancer. He would not promise me something and then suddenly take it away from me.

I am going to beat this. I am not going to die from this cancer. God will use my battle with cancer to bring others to Him, I thought.

"The fruit of the Spirit," wrote the apostle Paul to the church of Galatia, *"is love, joy, peace, patience, kindness, goodness, faithfulness, gentleness, self-control"* (Galatians 5:22–23).

"Lord," I prayed, "may the fruit of Your Spirit living with me be evident in my life as I seek to encourage and help others."

Theodore Mistra

God had put a couple of Bible verses on Martha's heart. She made note of them but didn't mention anything to me until after we found out about the cancer:

Do not fear, little flock, for it is your Father's good pleasure to give you the kingdom. (Luke 12:32)

If anyone is in Christ, he is a new creation; old things have passed away; behold, all things have become new. (2 Corinthians 5:17)

When she shared them with me later, they were sweet-tasting words; God used them to comfort both of us in the knowledge that He loved us.

God continued to show me that He was in control of my situation. Whenever a door closed, another door would open. In my hometown, my urologist could not accommodate my schedule; however, the doctors at the Mayo Clinic in Rochester, Minnesota, could. I believed the Mayo Clinic was where God was leading me.

Even though Dr. Baker was treating me with a vitamin infusion to strengthen me and help in recovery, we had both prayed about my treatment and were convicted that for my complete healing, I should have surgery at Mayo. It was more prudent to comply with the proven medical treatment rather than rely solely on an unproven pathway.

I also believed God was going to use my trial as a means for me to witness to others. I shared this belief—my vision—with Dr. Baker and with one of the employees at my company. They both saw this as well and encouraged me to share my situation with others.

Good friends surrounded me with wise counsel. Because they helped calm and soothe any anxiety I may have felt, I was able to maintain that deep sense of peace. I had no doubt that God had chosen me to experience this challenge so that I would draw closer to Him and share His love with others.

My wife Martha is a godly woman. The day after my diagnosis, during her personal prayer time, she sensed the Lord's assurance: "I have chosen your husband." This was an independent confirmation of the vision God had given me the day before when I first heard the startling news.

Rich, a consultant at my company and a good friend, offered, "Isaiah 49, verse 8, is especially for you."

*I will preserve you and give you
as a covenant to the people.*

*To restore the earth,
To cause them to inherit the desolate inheritance.*

Rich did not know that others had already encouraged me to encourage others to trust God as a result of my experience. "You are the one," he told me confidently. Two days later, another friend of mine, the head of a ministry, also shared Isaiah 49:8 with me. God was continuing to confirm His purpose for me in this battle with cancer.

One day as I read the Bible, this passage got my attention:

If you endure chastening, God deals with you as with sons; for what son is there whom a father does not chasten? But if you are without chastening, of which all have become partakers, then you are illegitimate and not sons. Furthermore, we have had human fathers who corrected us, and we paid them respect. Shall we not much more readily be in subjection to the Father of spirits and live? For they indeed for a few days chastened us as seemed best to them, but He for our profit, that we may be partakers of His holiness. Now no chastening seems to be joyful for the present, but painful; nevertheless, afterward it yields the peaceable fruit of righteousness to those who have been trained by it.

Therefore, strengthen the hands which hang down, and the feeble knees, and make straight paths for your feet, so that what is lame may not be dislocated, but rather be healed. (Hebrews 12:7–13)

I noted in my journal:

The discipline is for me to trust, and believe, that God has orchestrated all these events so that it glorifies Him. It is beyond description that at any earlier time in my life I was not ready. God has slowly prepared me, my heart, my faith, and my hope and placed His people around me to encourage, support, help, and heal me through His power and anointing. None of us would ever imagine such a trial and purpose; but everyone acknowledges this time, place, and trial.

I had no time to feel self-centered. The day I learned I had cancer I also learned that the spouse of one of my employees had terminal brain cancer. That certainly put my situation into perspective, quickly and humbly.

On another day I wrote:

Forgiveness. Conviction and repentance. Hopefully never again. Your iniquities and sins I will remember no more! Tricks of the mind: impulsive behavior, rationalization. Hold firm and steady. Weakness will prevail, but learn from them. Flesh or spirit confronts us daily. Experience teaches us to share with others.

We must believe God forgives and forgets with our true repentance. How do you know? You must let the guilt go from your heart and mind. When you sin, the Holy Spirit immediately convicts you of the sin. The Holy Spirit makes you aware of it deep in your consciousness. Your heart may tremble, your stomach may turn, you may have a sickening feeling, you may momentarily panic, or you may have a feeling of something washing over you from head to toe. That is the experience of the Holy Spirit speaking and acting through your consciousness.

For a mature Christian it happens instantly, immediately. It is rarely delayed. The impact is so fast that you have a tremendous self-consciousness. But it is at that precise time that you know you are His. He is one with you. The Spirit is an immediate, overpowering sense that shows you the truth. This spiritual intervention is God's love for us. He is perfecting us for His glory.

"Do not remember the former things, nor consider the things of old. Behold, I will do a new thing, now it shall spring forth; shall you not know it?" (Isaiah 43:18–19).

Focusing on past events, including sin, takes your heart away from looking to His glory and His purpose for us. Do not get consumed by guilt. God forgives and does not remember the past. So must we.

I received a postcard in the mail from a nonprofit ministry dedicated to restoring integrity and faith at work. Every month the ministry randomly selects and prays for people from their list of supporters and contributors. After they pray for the people, the ministry mails a postcard with a message, "You were prayed for today." My postcard was dated Monday, October 22. I received the postcard on Tuesday, October 23—the day the doctor informed me I had cancer.

The postcard confirmed that God had been with me from the beginning of my trial, before I ever knew what I would be facing. My name had not been selected two months or even one month prior to my diagnosis; nor was my name selected afterwards. My name had been selected in October, and the wonderful people at this ministry had prayed for me *the day before I learned about my diagnosis*—while the report was still sitting on the doctor's desk. I had not known the ministry was going to pray for me, and the ministry did not know I was going to have cancer. But God knew. He knew I would need those prayers and when. Those prayers were not a coincidence. The supernatural

SURROUNDED BY ANGELS

peace I felt immediately after the doctor informed me I had cancer was the result of those prayers. God's peace *would* sustain me through this battle.

Martha shared the word about my diagnosis with her prayer group. Within hours after the doctor told me I had cancer, intercessory prayer was taking place. So many faithful people were praying for me ... and I did not even know who they all were until Martha told me.

My peace came from God through the intercession of others. Even if I had felt fear that day instead of peace, people, nevertheless, were praying for me. But God *did* answer their prayers and I *did* know His peace from the beginning. It was definitely a peace that "passes all human understanding" (see Philippians 4:5–7).

Several days later God put on my heart and in my mind that my cancer was going to be a thorn in my side and that my journey was going to be a powerful statement to others.

Oswald Chambers[4] (1874–1917) was a Scottish minister and teacher who taught on the life of faith and abandonment to God. Martha read his collection of daily devotions, *My Utmost for His Highest*. The devotion for October 25 was based on John 15:16, where Jesus said:

> *You did not choose Me, but I chose you and appointed you that you should go and bear fruit, and that your fruit should remain, that whatever you ask the Father in My name He may give you.*

I realized my journey was not about me, but about glorifying God and loving and serving others. I only wished to share my trial so that others might see the light of Christ Jesus in me, and thirst for that same love.

In my scripture reading, I underlined additional verses that stood out for me:

> *In Christ Jesus you who once were far off have been brought near by the blood of Christ.* (Ephesians 2:13)

> *He Himself gave some to be apostles, some prophets, some evangelists, and some pastors and teachers, for the equipping of the saints for the work of ministry, for the edifying of the body of Christ, till we all come to the unity of the faith and of the knowledge of the Son of God, to a perfect man, to the measure of the stature of the fullness of Christ.* (Ephesians 4:11–13)

---

4 Actual person.

All things that are exposed are made manifest by the light, for whatever makes manifest is light. (Ephesians 5:13)

Take up the whole armor of God, that you may be able to withstand in the evil day, and having done all, to stand. (Ephesians 6:13)

I love that the armor of God protects me! I love the Holy Spirit within me!

As I wrote in my journal, I realized that much of what I was writing was repetitive, yet this was how everything occurred. Sometimes I would have the same fleeting thought, "Is this really God?"

But as God continued to remind me time and time again of His goodness, I finally surrendered. It *was* God, and this I knew.

3.
I WILL FOLLOW

*Your ears shall hear a word behind you, saying,
"This is the way, walk in it."*

Isaiah 30:21

Peace and purpose were what I had felt deeply after the doctor told me I had prostate cancer. This was not to say that I would not battle my own fear—the fear that comes from the flesh and from Satan—but I knew I was to be God's example, a witness to others to help them overcome *their* fear, and a fighter of the good fight.

I did not give myself time to feel self-pity or woe. I prayed that I would not be fearful, that I would be able to encourage others to take charge of their lives, to be aware of the dangers but to trust God with their own situations.

It wouldn't be long before the first opportunities came my way.

October 27. I had my first vitamin infusion at the clinic under the supervision of Dr. Baker. Of five patients being treated, I was the only man. The vitamin infusion would take about two hours, and I had no idea what to say to those four women during the lengthy procedure. I felt awkward being the only man, yet the women were all cordial and lighthearted toward me.

They talked among themselves about their children, their vacations, and their therapy. I could see that each of them had burdens of their own. My heart went out to all of them, and I wanted to encourage them. Had God chosen me to be there for those four women?

As I left, I said, "God bless all of you."

In my former life, I would have felt awkward offering a blessing to someone I hardly knew. That day, however, I felt freed to do so. Because we all shared this common denominator, our battle with cancer, I felt one with them.

Driving home, I wondered what would happen if I offered to have a Bible study with these women.

"Lord, is this my idea or Yours?" I prayed. "If it's Yours, direct me in this."

The next time I went for my vitamin infusion, I brought a Bible with me and, during our conversation, I shared a couple of passages that were meaningful promises to me amid the cancer. "Hey, this is like having our own support group!" one of them said, and the others agreed.

Soon we were introducing ourselves by name and revealing the type of cancer we each faced. "I have prostate cancer," I said without hesitation. A short time before, I doubt I would have had the courage to identify my cancer to a group of women. Fear or embarrassment would have prevented it. Yet the Spirit of Peace and the assurance that I was God's servant, a messenger of hope, was guiding me this day. I was trusting God, and He was enabling me to let my light shine.

I was receiving the infusion three times a week, and eventually (thank God) other men started showing up too.

Dr. Charles Stanley[5] is pastor of the First Baptist Church of Atlanta and founder of In Touch Ministries. I read his daily devotions, and one of Stanley's devotions during this time was another confirmation of God's purpose for me.

"If anyone serves Me, let him follow Me; and where I am, there My servant will be also. If anyone serves Me, him My Father will honor" (John 12:26).

At the time I noted in my journal:

- Do whatever God asks of you.
- Offer help wherever needed.
- Do good deeds at God's direction.

In another one of his daily devotions Dr. Stanley stated, "When the Lord wills for us to endure and overcome something that we would naturally seek to escape, *His directions are our prescriptions*. At such times, God has recognized a need in our lives that He can use only when we respond to His clear leading. But when we resist a difficult, divine assignment and give in to anxiety, fear, anger or bitterness, we rob ourselves of joy. The

---

5 Actual name.

pathway to our heart becomes blocked, our vitality and growth become strangled, and our testimony of Christ within us will become tragically obscured."

I knew God wanted me to experience love, joy, and peace and that I was to be His servant. I was not to run away and be self-absorbed. Rather, I was to serve and encourage others. By doing so, I believed God would bless and honor me and those around me whose lives I touched in this journey.

Martha and I intended to spend the day at an antique show. God, however, guided our footsteps in a different, and delightful, direction.

After we arrived at our destination, we discovered, to our surprise, that, in addition to the antique show, there was an art fair. The artists—all local artists—were cancer survivors. As I strolled through the many exhibits of artwork, I felt a connection with the artists, a sense of understanding, compassion, and peace that I'm sure I would not have experienced before my own diagnosis. I believed God had guided us to this place on this day.

A watercolor especially caught my attention. It was titled *Gentle Blow* and was a painting of a beautiful beach with blue skies, blue water, sand dunes, and greenery. As I enjoyed it, I felt a special sense of calm—and of hope. Would this watercolor uplift other cancer patients as much as it did me? I purchased the painting and arranged to have *Gentle Blow* displayed at the medical center for all to enjoy.

Another artist at the art fair created beautiful ceramic bowls inscribed with the Lord's Prayer. We purchased two of his pieces. The artist, and his mother who was with him, seemed touched that we liked his work. We encouraged the artist to continue using the gift God had given him.

At the art show, we also came across another beautiful painting of an ancient icon with flecks of 14-karat gold. The inscription on the painting was Jeremiah 29:11:

> *"I know the thoughts that I think toward you,"* says the Lord, *"thoughts of peace and not of evil, to give you a future and a hope."*

Seeing this inscription was actually the third time God brought it to my attention that week—the week my life changed forever.

We also met a talented photographer at the art fair, and she invited us to visit her home gallery. When we did, we saw a stunning photograph of a field of sunflowers. This beautiful photograph sparked a memory of a key decision in our lives twenty-one years earlier.

In the summer of 1986, I had been offered an opportunity to move to the Midwest. This would have been such a dramatic change in our lives that Martha and I decided to seek God's will by praying and asking Him for the answer in a powerful way. We needed a break to sort things out, so we took a vacation to Florida and took our three children with us, the youngest being only four months old.

Shortly after we reached our Florida destination, our four-month-old son started having difficulty breathing. We rushed him to the emergency room and learned he might have pneumonia.

While our son was being x-rayed, I was a nervous wreck. Completely restless, I started pacing around the waiting room. Needing something to occupy my mind, I picked up an old issue of *National Geographic*. The magazine was dated 1978, yet it was still on a table in the waiting room. The main article featured on the cover was about a Midwestern city noted for sunflowers.

Under the doctor's care our little boy recovered well, and we were able to enjoy the remainder of our mini-vacation. But that *National Geographic* article, published eight years before and left in the waiting room for me to pick up, stood out to Martha and me as we continued to process our decision. Through prayer and discussion, we concluded that it was another confirmation from God. With our three children we made the move—back to the Midwest.

Later, that day at the art show, Martha and I purchased that stunning photograph of the field of sunflowers. As we left the photographer's home gallery, the photographer commented that we had beautiful smiles and said, "Be well."

Be well. As we walked from the gallery to our car, Martha reflected, "That was a blessing from God. God imprinted that message on her heart to give to us." The thought gave me a sense of warmth, too, as God's graciousness flowed over me.

When the day began, we had had no idea that God would bless us in so many little ways that would mean such a great deal. I had known before, but had never realized in such meaningful ways, how much the Lord loves to surprise His people with blessings.

> *"My thoughts are not your thoughts, nor are your ways My ways,"* says the Lord. (Isaiah 55:8)

Isn't that the truth?

4.
THE SPIRIT WITHIN

*You will show me the path of life; in Your presence is fullness of joy;
at Your right hand are pleasures forevermore.*

Psalm 16:11

October 28. This morning as I began to awaken, the following thought flowed through my mind: *You are My chosen one with whom I am well pleased, worthy and respected.*

Wow! God was reassuring me that He and I were in this together. That He cared. That He had chosen me to bear this burden so that I, in turn, could tell others of His love and forgiveness. Through His Word, through the encouragement of my friends, and even through total strangers, God was flooding me with His presence. I was in awe!

Dr. Charles Stanley's devotion for this day said, in part, "We are to listen attentively for His call, and focus our minds and our hearts on obeying. Over time, the Spirit will bring forth 'fruit' in us, and draw us into unity of service with other believers."

I was already finding this to be so true in my life.

We are His workmanship, created in Christ Jesus for good works, which God prepared beforehand that we should walk in them. (Ephesians 2:10)

October 29. In my town there is a local group of Christian businessmen who share their faith and learn from each other—not only Christian truths, but also sound business principles. I have participated in their meetings as a guest speaker. As I prepared for another presentation, which I had titled "The Prodigal," I prayed that the Holy Spirit would speak through me so that I might encourage other fathers to always love, forgive, and be generous.

Theodore Mistra

I felt it was ironic that at previous times, while I was giving speeches, God had been working around or through me, taking me deeper into His Word while I trusted Him for all things to work out for good. He had brought me through trials at my company and with my children, and in my personal walk with Him. But as I focused more on God, I found myself becoming less me-centered. It had been a refining time, to be sure, and it's an ongoing journey.

But my personal trial now, the battle against cancer, was different. God was using me for His greater purpose, witnessing to others.

I have been crucified with Christ; it is no longer I who live, but Christ lives in me; and the life which I now live in the flesh I live by faith in the Son of God, who loved me and gave Himself for me. (Galatians 2:20)

Dr. Stanley's devotion for October 29 pointed out that "the only way to live the Christian life is to let the Holy Spirit live Christ's life through you. We make a commitment to God to surrender all that 'self' works, and seek only what He wants."

I noted in my journal:

The stages of a Christian life are salvation, service, dependence, and the exchanged life and then freedom and the joy of Christ in us! A deep peace that is unexplainable in human terms.

Throughout the day, I felt God's presence and continued to see signs that He would not forsake me or leave me.

That day I talked to a friend who had become particularly concerned after learning I had prostate cancer. He showed me such compassion and prayed a beautiful prayer for me. In his prayer, he referred to me as God's servant, and that God would use me to help others. At the time, he had no idea that other people had already shared the same message with me. This was yet another person affirming that God had a plan for me to glorify Him through this battle.

I believed God had brought all these people into my life over the past several years to provide me with support and encouragement during a time when I would really need them.

October 30. I gave my talk, "The Prodigal," to the Christian men's group. I based it on *The Return of the Prodigal Son,* by Henri J.M. Nouwen.[6] In summary, he said that everybody makes mistakes, but if someone makes a mistake and repents, it is up to

---

6 Actual name.

us to forgive and accept them back into the fold just as God forgives us through Jesus Christ. A father should always be willing to forgive a truly repentant child and welcome them back into his loving embrace.

After my talk, several individuals gathered around me to chat. One commented that a friend's wife had left her husband, but now she wanted to come back. The friend, who had been devastated by her departure, was uncertain what to do. Another person standing in our small circle said, "What would Christ do? If she truly repented, He would forgive her and welcome her back into the fold."

Later that day I met a friend who prayed for me. Afterward he reminded me about his own wife's battle with cancer. Upon learning that she had cancer, she had cried out, "Why, God? Why, God? Why, God?" Then a peace—the kind that transcends all understanding—had come over her, and she knew that God would be with her. She never lost that peace, and today her cancer is in remission. The "peace that passes all understanding," promised in Philippians 4:7, is real!

October 31. On a business trip to Europe, I took a quick nap on the flight to Chicago where I would make my flight connection. When I awoke, I was startled to see one of the flight attendants standing in the aisle, intently looking down at me with what I can only describe as compassion. She seemed to want to speak with me, but I could not imagine why.

"I'm sorry I don't know your arrival gate information yet," she apologized.

"No problem," I assured her.

She asked, "May I talk with you for a few minutes?"

I invited her into the vacant seat next to me, and she accepted. I'm not sure why—perhaps it was the small Bible I'd been reading before I took my nap. Spontaneously, she began telling me about two recent trips she had taken to Israel. The more she shared with me, the more enthused she became. Soon her energy became contagious, and I started feeling energized myself!

Almost nonstop, the flight attendant shared the joy she had experienced while visiting the places Jesus had walked. The one place that affected her life the most, she told me, was Jericho, the town where Zacchaeus had climbed a sycamore tree and waited for Jesus to walk by. "I wished I could have climbed that sycamore tree myself!" she exclaimed.

From our conversation, it had become clear to both of us that we were "brother and sister" in Christ. She was a Christ follower as I was. I told her, "I believe God wanted us to visit with each other."

"I believe that too," my new friend agreed. Then she told me, "I feel God is calling me to share the gospel with others who do not know Jesus Christ."

As I listened to what God was doing in her heart, I encouraged her to follow God's leading. I, too, felt compelled to share about my trial with cancer and how I believed God wanted to use me to help and encourage others.

She reached over and took my hand. "Can I pray for you?"

"I'd be honored," I replied. And we prayed together—two people who only moments before had been total strangers.

The young woman's prayer, so heartfelt and sincere for someone she had never met before, made my spirits soar. I then prayed for her, for God to clarify His call for her to share Christ with others. We were all smiles when we said, "Amen," and she rose to go back to work. I was at complete peace.

As I departed the plane, I gave her two copies of my book, *The Shepherd and His Staff*. Inside one copy I had inscribed, "To the angel God used to pray for me."

An angel indeed. The Holy Spirit within me felt renewed, and I knew God had sent this young woman my way to minister to my need and to remind me that all would be well with my life. I also felt assured that I had ministered to her as well. It was yet another confirmation that God was going to use me as a light to further glorify Him.

5.
A MESSAGE FROM GOD

Your word is a lamp to my feet and a light to my path.
Psalm 119:105

November 4. Upon my return from Europe, as I was changing planes at Chicago's O'Hare International Airport, I encountered another messenger from God.

In one of the terminals I noticed a woman standing opposite me. Although we did not exchange words, the encounter was something special. The woman was wearing a shirt that read, "Lost and Found, Luke 19:10." At the time, I could not remember the verse, yet I knew the message was for me. I later looked it up: *"The Son of Man has come to seek and to save that which was lost."*

I got home late that night, so I went straight to bed.

The next morning Martha's daily devotion was from Luke 19:10 which, interestingly, was also the chapter about Zacchaeus. I was stunned. It felt as if I was having an out-of-body experience!

When my trip had begun, a flight attendant had brought my attention to Zacchaeus. Back at O'Hare, a T-shirt had referred me to Luke 19:10 in God's Word. But that wasn't all. Upon arriving home, Martha also led me to the Zacchaeus story in the Bible.

It wasn't until then that I told her about the flight attendant and the woman at the airport. With a strange look on her face, Martha said, "At Wednesday's service we talked about Zacchaeus from Luke 19:10."

For a few quiet moments we pondered what had been unfolding before us. Finally, Martha spoke again.

"Zacchaeus means *righteous one*," she said.

She turned in her Bible to another verse that had been discussed at the Wednesday service: *"He* [God] *made Him* [Jesus] *who knew no sin to be sin for us, that we might become the righteousness of God in Him"* (2 Corinthians 5:21).

Martha went on to tell me that she believed God had chosen me for this battle because, with my faith in Him, I am declared a righteous person—that, even though I never would have expected to be afflicted with cancer, I was somebody whom God would use to glorify Himself through the faith and strength He was giving me along this journey. My job was to obey and submit to His will, even though I truly wished it were someone else!

Not a lightweight calling, by any means. I was sobered and humbled by Martha's faith that God would indeed work this together for good.

And references to Zacchaeus still did not end there. My daily meditation that morning from Dr. Charles Stanley's devotional was titled "Who Are the Lost?" and based on (you guessed it) Luke 19:1–26:

> *Jesus entered and passed through Jericho. Now behold, there was a man named Zacchaeus who was a chief tax collector, and he was rich. And he sought to see who Jesus was, but could not because of the crowd, for he was of short stature. So he ran ahead and climbed up into a sycamore tree to see Him, for He was going to pass that way. And when Jesus came to the place, He looked up and saw him, and said to him, "Zacchaeus, make haste and come down, for today I must stay at your house." So he made haste and came down, and received Him joyfully. But when they saw it, they all complained, saying, "He has gone to be a guest with a man who is a sinner."*
>
> *Then Zacchaeus stood and said to the Lord, "Look, Lord, I give half of my goods to the poor; and if I have taken anything from anyone by false accusation, I restore fourfold."*
>
> *And Jesus said to him, "Today salvation has come to this house, because he also is a son of Abraham; for the Son of Man has come to seek and to save that which was lost."*
>
> *Now as they heard these things, He spoke another parable, because He was near Jerusalem and because they thought the kingdom of God would appear immediately. Therefore He said: "A certain nobleman went into a far country to receive for himself a kingdom and to return. So he called ten of his servants, delivered to them ten minas, and said to them, 'Do business till I come.' But his citizens hated him, and sent a delegation after him, saying, 'We will not have this man to reign over us.'*
>
> *"And so it was that when he returned, having received the kingdom, he then commanded these servants, to whom he had given the money, to be called to him, that he might know how much every man had gained by trading. Then came the first, saying, 'Master, your mina has earned ten minas.' And he*

said to him, 'Well done, good servant; because you were faithful in a very little, have authority over ten cities.' And the second came, saying, 'Master, your mina has earned five minas.' Likewise he said to him, 'You also be over five cities.'

"Then another came, saying, 'Master, here is your mina, which I have kept put away in a handkerchief. For I feared you, because you are an austere man. You collect what you did not deposit, and reap what you did not sow.' And he said to him, 'Out of your own mouth I will judge you, you wicked servant. You knew that I was an austere man, collecting what I did not deposit and reaping what I did not sow. Why then did you not put my money in the bank, that at my coming I might have collected it with interest?'

"And he said to those who stood by, 'Take the mina from him, and give it to him who has ten minas.' (But they said to him, 'Master, he has ten minas.') For I say to you, that to everyone who has will be given; and from him who does not have, even what he has will be taken away from him."

In my journal later that day, I wrote:

It is not enough to follow Jesus in your head or your heart alone. You must show your faith by changed behavior. Zacchaeus showed his changed behavior by outward action. Zacchaeus did good works.

In the parable of the ten servants, the servants who multiplied the minas were rewarded with more. God gives us resources to use to build and expand His kingdom. We are expected to use our talents so they multiply and the kingdom grows. He asks each of us to account for what we do with His gifts to us. We must:

do good in all things,
bear fruit, and
praise God.

After I reread Luke 19:1–26, I felt a connection with the servants of the parable. Three things stood out to me. First, the fruits (gifts) that God has given me are to be used for His glory, not my own. Second, I want to honor God by the way I parent my children so that they gain a true picture of His love. And third, God wanted me to further glorify Him in the good works I do at my company.

Our responsibility is to minister to one another using the gifts God has given to us, so that His kingdom will grow.

November 5. As I continued to reflect on the meaning of Luke 19:1–10, I focused on how Christ followers show their faith. Most of us have faith in our minds and in our hearts, and even on our lips, but we must also express our faith in good works. We must have an impact on those within our spheres of influence and beyond.

Zacchaeus, in a sense, was a successful businessman. Yet, drawn to Jesus, Zacchaeus wanted to see Him desperately enough to climb a tree, and the moment Jesus called his name, Zacchaeus responded immediately and gladly.

When God calls us, we must not hesitate. We must respond to Him and submit to His will without reluctance. We must submit, responding with joy, not grudgingly, and with a sense of calling and purpose.

Even when others doubted Zacchaeus's intentions, he did not hesitate to invite Jesus into his home. That invitation is symbolic of accepting Jesus as Lord and Savior. Zacchaeus confessed his sins and repented by making a major sacrifice of his material possessions. He made a bold statement by accepting Christ immediately and gladly and then giving generously of his wealth without hesitation.

When we accept Jesus, we have a responsibility to then reflect His character in our everyday lives. *"We are his workmanship, created in Christ for good works which God prepared beforehand that we should walk in them"* (Ephesians 2:10).

6.
TENDING MY FLOCK

*Shepherd the flock of God which is among you,
serving as overseers, not by compulsion but willingly,
not for dishonest gain but eagerly.*

1 Peter 5:2

November 7. I gave my testimony to another local men's group composed of Christian businessmen, and I spoke about shepherd leadership. I felt the Spirit anoint me and speak words of conviction and encouragement through me.

It is always a blessing for me to bear witness of what God is doing in my life and how He has led me through various trials and life-changing situations. And I sense that whenever I share my testimony with others, my story is also a blessing to those who hear. Perhaps one of my stories is similar to what they're going through that day and they're comforted to know that they're not alone. Or maybe God is using a lesson He taught me, or a scripture that resonated with me in the situation I'm describing, to minister to someone in the audience who's walking a similar journey.

Later that day, a former pastor of mine visited me at my office. He had heard that I had cancer. We talked about the challenge of battling cancer and about the purpose of the battle that God was revealing to me. My friend offered a beautiful prayer for me, calling on the healing power of God and rebuking Satan in the name of Jesus.

By His wounds we are healed. (Isaiah 53:5 NIV and see 1 Peter 2:24)

I have always felt it important to stay in touch with the staff at my company, to get a sense of how they're doing and feeling and to know what some of their issues are.

Nearly every day, I make it a point to walk through the campus in the morning and then again in the afternoon. Management gurus call this MWA, or "management by walking around."

As I made my rounds this day, greeting and talking with some of my employees, one shared with me how she was struggling to cope with the recent loss of her aunt. "My aunt was a strong believer," she said.

I could see pain in her eyes and that she needed a word of hope and encouragement.

"What expression would your aunt have on her face right now?" I asked.

"She believed in heaven, and she would have a smile on her face."

I said, "Keep picturing your aunt in heaven with a smile on her face."

A smile came on my employee's face, and the expression in her eyes seemed to transform from pain to joy.

Those who have not accepted Christ as Lord and Savior may not believe such a mental picture to be valid. But this woman's deceased aunt *had* trusted Christ, and now her niece could forever envision her aunt in heaven with a smile on her face.

Again, God used the greater need of another person to help me focus on Him and on His other children. It reminded me that everyone is hurting one way or another, and my cancer was not just about me. God was using it to make me more sensitive to the needs of others, to move me from self-centeredness to a spirit of empathy.

> *...that their hearts may be encouraged, being knit together in love, and attaining to all riches of the full assurance of understanding, to the knowledge of the mystery of God, both of the Father and of Christ.* (Colossians 2:2)

The visit with my grieving employee turned out to be a blessing for both of us. God's purpose was again confirmed, that I am to be a giver of encouragement and hope to others. I'm finding that the words of Romans 12:10–12 are continually penetrating my spirit, directing my future profoundly while maturing me in the faith:

> *Be kindly affectionate to one another with brotherly love, in honor giving preference to one another; not lagging in diligence, fervent in spirit, serving the Lord; rejoicing in hope, patient in tribulation, continuing steadfastly in prayer.* (Romans 12:10–12)

Before the cancer, I knew that God was calling me to trust Him even more—that He would be shifting me into another phase of life even better and more productive than my life to date. I had had this growing conviction for several years. I just didn't know the details—until the cancer.

As they say, I'm now a bit older and wiser—and grayer. As He did with many of the Bible's prophets and kings, God calls each of us only when we are ready. Abraham, Moses, Noah, and Solomon all had the greatest impact in their later years.

Little did I know how much God would allow and orchestrate my life's trials and opportunities to further His kingdom—until the cancer.

7.
IN GOD'S HANDS

As for me, I trust in You, O Lord;
I say, "You are my God."
My times are in your hand.

Psalm 31:14–15

November 9. After a diagnosis of cancer, it is suggested that a full body scan be done to determine whether the cancer has spread to other areas of the body.

As the times for my CAT and PET scans approached, I admit that I grew a bit nervous.

"Fill me with Your peace, Lord," I asked. "You're in control, I'm not. I place myself in Your loving arms."

When I met the nurse who was going to give me my PET scan, she mentioned that she had previously worked in the cardiovascular unit at another hospital with one of the cardiologists there.

"I did a cardio stress test on a senior executive from your company several years ago," she recalled.

"I was that senior executive!" I acknowledged. "How do you remember such an impression from so long ago?"

"Because I remember him being a kind and nice person," she replied.

It was another humbling moment. I had no idea that I had made such a positive impression on this nurse so many years ago. It was as though God opened yet another door to His lovingkindness. He knew that I'd be a little anxious today, and He brought this kind nurse—another angel—back into my path for the support I needed.

Other than the prostate, the result of the body scan was normal.

"Thank You, Lord, for this encouraging news!"

November 10. I reflected on the fact that Dr. Baker had suggested the scan and had sent me to a hospital that was only one of two in the nation specifically programmed for prostate cancer. I was one of the first patients in the U.S. to utilize this novel technology. I pondered the odds of that, thankful that God had opened yet another door through one of his angels, Dr. Baker.

In a sense, it almost felt surreal.

"Why me?" I asked myself.

It was humbling how God was so obviously going before me in my journey.

I wrote in my journal:

No matter how difficult this may be, I must be patient in affliction, and let it evolve one day at a time, being joyful, hopeful, and faithful in prayer. In all things, I must do well, and bear fruit in God's glory.

We know that all things work together for good to those who love God, to those who are the called according to His purpose. For whom He foreknew, He also predestined to be conformed to the image of His Son, that He might be the firstborn among many brethren. (Romans 8:28–29)

I wrote: As I undergo this life-transforming experience, I see God in every event and situation. The resources and the people He has surrounded me with are clear signs that He is in control, that He is equipping and empowering me to be His witness to His glory as I fulfill His plan.

Most assuredly, I say to you, whatever you ask the Father in My name He will give you (John 16:23).

These things I [Jesus] have spoken to you, that in Me you may have peace. In the world you will have tribulation; but be of good cheer, I have overcome the world (John 16:33).

November 12. It the midst of my trial God called Martha and me to be encouragers to others in need. We prayed and counseled a friend of ours about his family and married life. He was in a terrible state of mind, completely distraught. When he called us early in the morning, I was doing my Bible study and knew that his was a cry for help.

SURROUNDED BY ANGELS

It would have been easy for us to withdraw from life and to focus exclusively on our own problems, yet that was not what God intended for us to do. Rather, we were to be His witnesses and bear fruit for others. We listened to his story, offered encouraging words, and prayed intently with him.

November 13. While reading 2 Chronicles 20 last evening I was reminded that King Jehoshaphat was a faithful and fruitful man, and when faced with battle he called to God in prayer. The Lord answered, "The battle is not yours, but God's." But King Jehoshaphat did not sit back and do nothing. God made it clear that Jehoshaphat had to prepare for the battle, so he diligently equipped his army and marched to war. When God told Jehoshaphat to stand firm and watch the deliverance the Lord would give him, he obeyed. Even though he was prepared to fight and win the battle on his own, he stood still and watched how God caused the destruction of his enemies.

"Do not be afraid or dismayed," God assured him. "Tomorrow go out against them, for the LORD is with you" (verses 15, 17).

I was starting to feel anxious about the next day's visit with the surgeon at the Mayo Clinic. But reading this portion of biblical history calmed my spirit. Through Jehoshaphat's story, God commanded me not to be afraid or discouraged—that I was to go out and face tomorrow boldly, for the Lord would be with me. God was telling me that He would be with me at the Mayo Clinic; that I was not to be afraid or discouraged.

On a personal basis, God surrounded me with His army of supporters and encouragers. God gave me access to a powerful army that He would use to help me face and win my battle with cancer.

November 14. Martha and I visited the surgeon, Dr. Peterson, at the Mayo Clinic in Rochester. I prayed for peace and for clarity and confirmation of God's will.

God was faithful, and I indeed experienced His continuing supernatural peace.

While I was walking through the Mayo hallways and subways, I marveled how the two hospitals (Rochester Methodist Hospital and Saint Mary's Hospital) had come together more than a hundred years ago to serve the community. Because the two hospitals truly serve others, I believe God has blessed the Mayo Clinic in Rochester, Minnesota. As we walked about the campus, I felt a genuine sense of goodness within me, a confidence that God has blessed this place of care and healing.

It is important that you understand this was my experience at the time. I am completely confident that God has blessed and gifted many other hospitals and doctors to bring healing to His people. Mayo was just a pathway to healing for me; it does not mean it is yours. You must find your own pathway that is ordered by God.

> *Behold, I will bring it health and healing; I will heal them and reveal to them the abundance of peace and truth.* (Jeremiah 33:6)

Indeed the Lord was with me, and at a time and place Martha and I had least expected to feel His presence. As we were leaving, we got off the elevator to pass through the lobby of the clinic building and heard somebody playing "On Eagle's Wings" on the piano. This song by Michael Joncas[7] is one of Martha's favorite Christian songs, so she paused and started to sing the words.

We both felt uplifted, and tears of joy filled our eyes. It was God affirming that He is always with us! We were nearly overwhelmed with emotion. We went back to find the piano player, but the seat at the piano was empty.

Was the piano player a messenger from God? Why was he playing that particular song, something Martha and I so needed to hear at that time? Why had we taken that specific elevator to exit the clinic? (The clinic had many elevators near many other exits....)

Once again, God had clearly confirmed His presence.

> *"Call to Me [God], and I will answer you, and show you great and mighty things, which you do not know."* (Jeremiah 33:3)

As we were driven to the airport, Martha and I discussed how God is watching over me. The driver overheard our discussion and asked if we were Christians. He said he was a Christian and suggested I read about healing in Jeremiah. When we got to the airport, he asked if he could pray with us; the three of us held hands and prayed. What a blessed time!

November 15. I shared with a friend what Martha and I had experienced at the Mayo Clinic. My friend noted, "I've been praying Psalm 91:11 specifically for you every day." She quoted the verse to me: *"He shall give His angels charge over you, to keep you in all your ways."*

Again, I was stunned by God's goodness. Although I had not known that this friend had been praying for me, I believe the piano player at the Mayo Clinic, as well as the taxi driver, *truly were* messengers from God in answer to my friend's prayer.

---

7 Actual name.

Indeed, I was in God's hands! I was never alone. I was continuously surrounded by His angels. Even if they did not know it, God asked them in His time to share His words with me, His servant.

8.
THE ARMOR OF GOD

It is God who arms me with strength,
and makes my way perfect.

Psalm 18:32

November 16. Last night I talked with the employee at my company whose husband had terminal brain cancer. Her husband's situation gave me a different perspective on what I was experiencing. I offered to help in any way I could.

I reflected on the Bible passage on bearing fruit in all we do. If we are to be "imitators of Christ," it is required of us to do good things for others. Sometimes we do good deeds because we feel compelled to do so, or because doing a good deed makes us feel good, or perhaps because we know doing a good deed is the right thing to do. As Christians, we should always be cheerful givers, never expecting anything in return. If, indeed, the Holy Spirit dwells within us, we should do good deeds with sincerity, reflecting "all" the fruit from the Spirit inside us. It is the "Golden Rule":

Whatever you want men to do to you, do also to them. (Matthew 7:12)

November 17. Today I shared with my friend, the fellow believer who had recently undergone surgery for prostate cancer, some of the "God incidents" I had experienced during the past three weeks.

"Although I feel a sense of peace now," I reflected, "I don't think I would have been spiritually mature enough to handle this situation twelve or even six months ago."

I believed my journey was on God's timeline. Any earlier, and I would not have seriously considered using vitamin infusions as an integral part of my cancer treatment. Nor would I have had access to the new radiology technology (the scan specifically programmed for prostate cancer). It was a convergence of events that could only have been orchestrated by God, at His time for His purpose.

My friend nodded his head with a big smile on his face. "I know. I understand," he said.

And he did. He understood. He was a survivor. He fought his battle and now was encouraging me to fight my own.

I still marvel at the support group God surrounded me with, most of whom I never knew or thought I would ever need to know. Yet God knew. God provided me with everything I needed, and I was comforted knowing that He was present in every event.

Our bodies are the temples of the Holy Spirit. As such, we are to honor and protect our bodies, both physically and spiritually. This requires us to take care of our bodies, and to remain healthy so we are able to do His will and purpose for us. We are to be active in seeking solutions to our physical health. We're to depend on God to lead us to His path for our healing.

> *I beseech you therefore, brethren, by the mercies of God, that you present your bodies a living sacrifice, holy, acceptable to God, which is your reasonable service. And do not be conformed to this world, but be transformed by the renewing of your mind, that you may prove what is that good and acceptable and perfect will of God.*
>
> *For I say, through the grace given to me, to everyone who is among you, not to think of himself more highly than he ought to think, but to think soberly, as God has dealt to each one a measure of faith.* (Romans 12:1–3)

I continued writing:

As believers, we need to put on the full armor of God, the armor that will withstand Satan. That would withstand anxiety, doubt, worry and fear.

> *My brethren, be strong in the Lord and in the power of His might. Put on the whole armor of God, that you may be able to stand against the wiles of the devil. For we do not wrestle against flesh and blood, but against principalities, against powers, against the rulers of the darkness of this age, against spiritual hosts of wickedness in the heavenly places. Therefore take up the whole armor of God, that you may be able to withstand in the evil day, and having done all, to stand.*

Stand therefore, having girded your waist with truth, having put on the breastplate of righteousness, and having shod your feet with the preparation of the gospel of peace; above all, taking the shield of faith with which you will be able to quench all the fiery darts of the wicked one. And take the helmet of salvation, and the sword of the Spirit, which is the word of God; praying always with all prayer and supplication in the Spirit, being watchful to this end with all perseverance and supplication for all the saints—and for me, that utterance may be given to me, that I may open my mouth boldly to make known the mystery of the gospel, for which I am an ambassador in chains; that in it I may speak boldly, as I ought to speak. (Ephesians 6:10–20)

The armor of God: Salvation, righteousness, truth, the gospel, faith, and the Word.

November 18. One of the men at the infusion clinic was undergoing hormone therapy at the same time I was receiving vitamin infusions. He was a farmer in his seventies and liked to tell stories about farming in the Midwest.

After being diagnosed with prostate cancer, he had started reading books on the subject to educate himself. He recommended *Surviving Prostate Cancer* by Patrick Walsh, M.D.[8] Or at least I thought he did. That weekend I bought a copy of the book. The author answered many of the questions I had been asking myself. His answers were a comfort and actually kept me from fretting about my own health. Patrick Walsh was compassionate on the matter and simple to understand.

After I finished reading the book, I brought it with me to the infusion clinic on a day I knew my farmer friend would be there.

"Thank you for suggesting this book," I said. "It was really a revelation to me. Would you like to read it again?"

"Yes, I would," he said, and I handed him the book.

A puzzled look came over his face. "This isn't the book I read. I don't think I've heard of this author."

My friend was in his seventies; maybe he was starting to become forgetful. "What book *did* you suggest I read?" I probed.

"It was a smaller book, by a fellow with another name," he replied.

Then what prompted me to seek a book by Dr. Walsh? I wondered to myself. I had known of the name—Walsh; he was one of the prominent specialists in prostate cancer. But I had no idea he had written a book about prostate cancer. I had looked for a book

---

8 Actual name.

by Walsh on the subject because I thought my farmer friend had suggested I read it. Was this a misunderstanding on my part, or was it the work of the Holy Spirit?

Dr. Baker was surprised when I shared the misunderstanding with her. She knew that Dr. Patrick Walsh was the surgeon at Johns Hopkins Hospital who had pioneered the nerve-sparing prostatectomy, which is now the standard for prostate cancer surgery. However, she did not know that Walsh had written a book on prostate cancer. I believed this was another indication from God that He was guiding me and that I was to have prostate surgery as another integral part of my pathway to healing.

It is only by God's grace that I am able to hold firm and steadfast. Paraphrasing 1 Peter 5:10, "After you have struggled awhile, He will come and make you firm, strong, and steadfast."

When I am looking for some sign of His presence and guidance in my immediate surroundings, He often reminds me of a sign He gave me previously, which I forgot or missed. And I take comfort in that, for His Word says *"the same yesterday, today, and forever"* (Hebrews 13:8).

November 19. The more I read and meditate on the Bible, the more I realize that God's Word is our guide for life. It has everything we need to be righteous, successful people, obedient to His will and purpose.

> *All Scripture is given by inspiration of God, and is profitable for doctrine, for reproof, for correction, for instruction in righteousness, that the man of God may be complete, thoroughly equipped for every good work.* (2 Timothy 3:16–17)

November 20. As I sit in the infusion clinic, I feel empathy and compassion for each of the patients. Most, if not all, have advanced cancer. This is their hope for life. Sometimes I just want to reach out and heal them. I pray for each of them.

I also have been praying about my healing. As the Bible teaches, the body is the temple of the Holy Spirit. The temple is holy. Anyone who invades the body will be cast out. I pray for the cancer to be cast out. This is a prayer of faith that calls out for a higher power to heal. There have been numerous studies claiming the power of positive thinking. *Faith* is the ultimate power!

> *Strengthened with all might, according to His glorious power, for all patience and longsuffering with joy; giving thanks to the Father who has qualified us to be partakers of the inheritance of the saints in the light. He has delivered us from the power of darkness and conveyed us into the kingdom of the Son of His love, in whom we have redemption through His blood, the forgiveness of sins.* (Colossians 1:11–14)

9.
WHERE GOD LEADS

*I will instruct you and teach you in the way you should go;
I will guide you with my eye.*

Psalm 32:8

November 21. In the holiday tradition of Thanksgiving, we remember our blessings and give thanks to God, praising and worshipping Him. *Give thanks in all things … do good in all things.*

Cancer frightens people; yet for some of us, cancer can also be a life-transforming experience, actually improving one's quality of life. When we reflect on our life and priorities, a change takes place. We acquire a deep, ongoing peace within us that nobody can explain.

A difficult challenge for me along the way was whom I could or should open up to and share my trial with them. On one hand, the more people who knew, the more people who would pray for me and offer me encouragement. On the other hand, not everyone understands or empathizes with one who is traveling this path. Many are afraid of contracting the disease themselves; many don't know what to say or fear saying the wrong thing; others just don't want to be "pulled down" by another's trial.

I did not want to devote my time or effort to those who I felt would either not understand or not want to come alongside me in prayer and encouragement. The only people I wanted to share this journey with were those I knew would be fruitful around me—sincere, truly caring, wanting to help in any way they could.

I was not trying to hide my cancer. I simply did not want my cancer to become a topic among those who did not know me well or understand the journey I had to travel. I prayed for discernment and that I would say and do what the Lord required of me whenever I interacted with others.

Do not be unwise, but understand what the will of the Lord is. And do not be drunk with wine, in which is dissipation; but be filled with the Spirit. (Ephesians 5:17–18)

Let us hold fast the confession of our hope without wavering, for He who promised is faithful. (Hebrews 10:23)

Throughout Scripture God promises us many things for those who believe in Jesus Christ. Many times, we hear about people who pray, and their prayers, at least for them, go unanswered. If this was true then we must ask ourselves, why do we have so many people being saved, not only now but also in the past? Something must have impacted them. As a matter of fact, our faith would not have continued to multiply if God did not keep His promises to us. The fact that Christian faith has multiplied is clear evidence of God's goodness and dependability. He is the same yesterday, today, and tomorrow. Why else would people remain hopeful and trust in Him if they had not been witnesses of His goodness, grace, and mercy?

One day I claimed God's promise of a long life for me. I had mentioned earlier that, several months before I learned I had cancer, I had felt a conviction in my heart that over the next twenty-five years—between ages sixty and eighty-five—I would be more fruitful for the kingdom than I had been earlier in my life.

I discussed this with a friend of mine. "When I was in my thirties and forties, I wanted to be a young superstar, yet God had another plan for me. His plan was for me to be more fruitful in my later years." Biblical characters such as Moses, Noah, and Abraham were in their eighties and nineties when God called them to advance the kingdom.

My friend said, "It's good for me to hear your strong conviction. Life does go on for those who are called to His purpose."

We are to pray and glorify God continually in all things during our life on earth. We must give thanks in all things, good and bad.

As Rick Warren[9] states in his book, *The Purpose Driven Life,* we must shift our focus to worshipping God and helping others. Life is not about us, it is about worshipping Him; and when we do worship God and help others, we will have a deep sense of satisfaction, peace, and joy. We will then grow in maturity and have an effect on others for their good and for the glory of God.

God gives wisdom and knowledge and joy to a man who is good in His sight. (Ecclesiastes 2:26)

I am not ashamed of the gospel of Christ, for it is the power of God to salvation for everyone who believes, for the Jew first and also for the Greek. For in it the righteousness of God is revealed from faith to faith; as it is written, "The just shall live by faith." (Romans 1:16–17)

The things which are impossible with men are possible with God. (Luke 18:27)

November 23. I continue to marvel at how God had orchestrated the network of people who surrounded and encouraged me from the beginning of my battle.

Last week I could not receive my vitamin infusion because my veins were no longer able to sustain the vein punctures. Another option was to have a catheter inserted into my arm; however, no one on the clinic's staff was qualified to do this procedure and no one could be located to do so. (It was the day before Thanksgiving, the clinic was understaffed, and nobody was responding to the pages.) Although the lack of response surprised me, I was relieved as well. I was a little worried about somebody inserting a catheter into my arm at the clinic.

The staff scheduled me for one the following Monday. I thought about this over Thanksgiving and still felt uneasy about waiting until Monday. So on Friday morning, the day after Thanksgiving, I called a friend who is also a doctor.

"By any chance would you know someone who could insert a catheter in my arm?" I asked.

He said, "I'll check, but today you have only a 50 percent chance of getting in. We are on reduced staff because of the holiday."

Well, God knew my chances would be a lot higher. Within fifteen minutes, my friend called back. "I've got someone if you can come to the hospital right now."

---
9 Actual name.

The staff at the hospital was so attentive and gracious to do this for me when they were understaffed the day after Thanksgiving. I felt completely at peace, knowing that this was what God had wanted me to do.

After I registered at the front desk, I noticed a plaque on the wall with the hospital's mission statement:

"Improving Health Through Christian Service."

Over the past twenty years I have made numerous visits to that hospital, but never before had I noticed that plaque. I did not need to ask why I noticed the plaque for the first time now. I already knew that God's hand was guiding all the events throughout my trial, no matter how small, and He had opened my eyes to the hospital's mission statement on this day.

I never second-guess the direction the Holy Spirit prompts me to go. I go on faith and with confidence. The hospital where I will have my surgery will not be my decision to make. The decision will be God's, and I will know what His decision is when He reveals it to me. And when He does, I will embrace His will and step out on faith.

I know when the Holy Spirit is speaking to me. In my case, it's almost as if I feel myself rising from my body—as if I am having an out-of-body experience—and then I feel myself gliding along a path, a path I know God has prepared for me. This has been my personal experience, and I've found it reliable. This is what I feel when the Holy Spirit is speaking to me.

Other believers have confirmed that this is so. They claim we will know God is working in our lives in a very powerful and visible manner.

God knows I do not question the power of the Holy Spirit inside me. I take one step at a time, praying and seeking His will; and when I feel that inner peace, I know—without a doubt—that God has made His will clear to me. I pray that someday my journey of faith will be an inspiration to others and bring them the peace of God that transcends all human understanding.

I thought about the other two men who were receiving treatment for prostate cancer at the infusion clinic. Each was in his seventies, and each had chosen a different form of treatment in addition to their vitamin infusions. One, the farmer who had recommended a book to me, had chosen hormone therapy; the other had chosen radiation treatments.

What was the probability that these two gentlemen were receiving vitamin infusions for prostate cancer at the same time and place that I was receiving vitamin infusions? Was God confirming that my path to healing was to be surgery, while theirs was to be hormone therapy and radiation treatments? We are to seek God's guidance for healing, not resting until we have a sense of peace. I prayed that God would heal and bless both men with a long life.

> [Jesus speaking] *"Peace I leave with you, My peace I give to you; not as the world gives do I give to you. Let not your heart be troubled, neither let it be afraid."* (John 14:27)

> [Jesus speaking] *"Let not your heart be troubled; you believe in God, believe also in Me.* (John 14:1)

10.
ON EAGLE'S WINGS

Those who wait on the Lord
shall renew their strength;
they shall mount up with wings like eagles.

Isaiah 40:31

One day as Martha was perusing her email, she received one that she felt was meant for me. There was no return address that we could readily find, so we could not thank the sender for such a timely word of encouragement. It was another God incident of a messenger with a message for us. It blessed us, and I pray it blesses you. Enjoy it!

THE EAGLE

The eagle is a symbol used many times in Scripture; in fact, it is mentioned thirty-eight times throughout the Bible. We can learn some important lessons from this majestic creation of God. Eagles have a wingspan of two meters and are approximately 90 cm tall. The eagle mates for life and uses the same nest for life. This nest is built in a safe place, often on the ledge of a sharp cliff. It is built to last, and the largest nest reported is 9½ feet wide and 20 feet deep.

When the babies are born, both parents assume responsibility for their care. They are gentle parents. The parents bring food up to the nest and feed the eaglets small pieces of meat. Within forty-five days they can weigh nearly forty times their birth weight. At three months, they get special feathers for flying—and a new learning experience begins. The mother eagle flies into the nest and begins to thrash around, causing a great commotion. Eventually one of the eaglets will fall from the nest and begin heading for the earth below. Never having used his wings before, he is not really sure what to do, but he does do lots of flapping while heading straight down! Just before he hits the ground, the mother eagle flies underneath in order to catch the baby on her powerful wings, and she flies him safely back to the nest. This continues day after day until all the eaglets learn to fly.

There are two verses in Scripture that actually mention this routine of the eagle. In Deuteronomy 32:10–11, Moses reminds the children of Israel how God cared for them and guarded them just "like an eagle that stirs up its nest and hovers over its young, that spreads its wings to catch them and carries them on its pinions." Again, in Exodus 19:4, God says, "He will carry the children of Israel on eagles' wings." We can get very comfortable in our "nest"—with our way of doing things, our way of thinking, our opinions, our "comfort zones." Then when God comes and "stirs up our nest" we get upset. We do not always identify this as a growing experience. Sometimes, if we're really honest, we really do not want to stretch and grow beyond what's become "normal" or "comfortable." We get complacent and satisfied with where we are, and any interruptions are viewed as negative. But God wants us to soar, to become all that He created us to become. He never stirs up our nest without good reason!

The eagle can see a rabbit two miles away. It can soar up to two miles above the ground and fly at speeds of up to 100 miles per hour. It has a separate eyelid that slides across the eye sideways in order to keep the eye clean and free from dust as it flies. Its bones are hollow and, therefore, it is light of frame. It has cross ribs like steel bars in skyscrapers. The eagle has 7000 feathers. The back feathers are as long as the head feathers. Its beak is black until it reaches three years of age, and then it turns golden.

When eagles are about 30 years old, they go through a renewal process. They find a secret place high in the mountains and begin to tear out the feathers that have been damaged over the years. The eagle bleeds badly, but this procedure is necessary for the eagle to renew its strength. If it did not do this, it would not be able to live its normal 60 years.

Referring to God's love for His children, Psalm 103:5 says, "who satisfies your desires with good things so that your youth is renewed like the eagle's." Just like the majestic eagle, a time of renewal is necessary for every child of God. A time when we get rid of what is weighing us down, holding us back, aging us spiritually. A time to give up sinful habits, to give in to the Holy Spirit in whatever way He is convicting us. We need to do this even if the time of renewal is painful! Some things we hold on to so tightly that to let go actually causes us pain. But in order to have the long, powerful, useful spiritual life that God plans for us, we need to do just that. It will renew our spiritual youthfulness.

When an eagle is held in captivity, it can become one of the dirtiest of birds. But when the eagle is free to soar in God's creation, it is the cleanest of birds. It was created to be free, to soar to great heights. It was never meant to remain close to the earth in the lowlands; it was created to soar.

Likewise, God has created us to remain pure and holy and conformed to His image. He has created us to soar. Do not allow the freedom we have in Him to be compromised by spending too much time in worldly thinking, activities, and mindsets. Remain clean and soar!

An eagle does not fly like other birds; it flaps its wings only occasionally. Flapping its wings continuously like other birds would burn up incredible amounts of strength and endurance; the eagle would require much more food for fuel if it did not soar. Instead, it sits on a high ledge and waits for the right wind currents to come. When the time is right, it launches out, catches the current, and soars upward. It is nearly effortless because the eagle has waited for the right time. There is a special "upgoing" wind that it rides as it circles higher and higher in the sky.

What a lesson for God's children! How often do we waste strength by jumping out too soon and "flapping our wings" instead of waiting for God's timing? Waiting is not a popular concept in these days of instant everything. But when we wait on the Lord—wait for His timing, for His answers, for His direction—then we can soar to new heights and fly to new places.

Those who wait on the Lord *will renew their strength, they will soar on wings like eagles: they will run and not grow weary, they will walk and not faint.* (Isaiah 40:28–31)

May your troubles be less, your blessings be more, and nothing but happiness come through your door.

November 25. Martha went online and found the song "On Eagle's Wings" by Michael Joncas. This was the song that had ministered so richly to us at the Mayo Clinic. Listening to the music and the words was a blessing for both of us. The song brought tears of peace and joy to us as we both felt God's love all around us.

When I heard the verse, I wept:

*To His angels He's given a command
to guard you in all of your ways,
upon their hands they will bear you up,
lest you dash your foot against a stone* (Psalm 91:11–12).

I wrote in my journal:

Ever since I heard "On Eagle's Wings" composed by Michael Joncas, at the Mayo Clinic nearly two weeks ago, it seemed God had been opening doors for me, making the right people available all around me. God had been my provider in all things. No matter what medical facility I was in for treatment, God surrounded me with a marvelous medical staff that was as compassionate as they were professional. The people at these medical facilities provided me with a tremendous sense of security. Whether they knew it or not, they were the angels God had commanded to guard me. God is my rock and refuge in whom I trust. He is always with me.

No one has seen God at any time. If we love one another, God abides in us, and His love has been perfected in us. (1 John 4:12)

November 26. Yesterday, while I was at the clinic receiving another infusion of vitamins, I had the opportunity to engage in conversation with some of the other patients. I felt that God was opening opportunities for me to share my faith. As I interacted with the other patients, I prayed that God would bless our growing relationship for His good. I am His servant.

"You did not choose Me, but I chose you and appointed you that you should go and bear fruit, and that your fruit should remain, that whatever you ask the Father in My name He may give you." (John 15:16)

November 27. Last night I struggled with falling asleep. In the morning I felt tired, as if I had been awake all night.

Around 7:30 A.M., a friend called, desperately needing to talk with me. "God led me to 2 Timothy 2:24–26 and 3:1–7," he said.

My friend was struggling spiritually over his relationship with his wife. I knew he needed some encouragement. We spent time discussing Scripture and his role as the head of his family, protecting them from evil through the power of God.

After our discussion, I felt my service to God was somewhat ironic. For years I have shared with others that I believed God had called me to mentor other men in business and in parenting. Today, however, I counseled a friend in marriage at a time when I was battling cancer. God did not want me to be self-absorbed in my own trial. He had chosen me to be a light to the world and to bear fruit. We are to be obedient to Christ by loving and serving others in all that we do. Who am I to question or doubt what God brings my way?

November 28. I shared the lyrics to "On Eagle's Wings" with my friend Rich.

"Yes-s-s-s!" my friend responded upon hearing the words. Indeed, God had sent me those lyrics for this time in my life.

I also shared the lyrics with another friend. He radiated a bright, wonderful smile of awe on his face. I knew God was using my battle with cancer for His purpose to glorify Him.

11.
SERVING OTHERS

*I will bless the LORD who has given me counsel;
my heart also instructs me in the night seasons.*

Psalm 16:7

November 29. While I was at the infusion clinic, I provided information to another patient who was also receiving treatment for cancer. Although he did not have prostate cancer, I encouraged him to research the material. I also offered to help him in any way I could. This was another way of serving others.

November 30. Martha and I, with all three of our children, went to visit my mother and a few other relatives. While there, I did not tell anyone else of my illness because I didn't want them to be worrying about me. Although they would have prayed for me, I would not have been at peace if they knew. I felt comfortable with those who already knew, and with those whom I felt God had led me to be open with. If I did share my battle with anyone else during this time, it would be because God had clearly impressed upon me to do so.

Only when my journey was over would I share my story with others—and only in God's time. Other cancer patients might have a desire to share their trial for whatever reason, but I did not. Instead, I continued to praise, and glorify God for all the blessings I had already received from my experience, and for all the blessings I would still receive. I want to be truly fruitful while I patiently trust in God.

On the plane flying home, I looked out the window and saw a beautiful rainbow. I took this as a sign—my personal promise from God—that He would never leave or forsake me.

My two sons commented to me that they appreciated my decision to move to the Midwest where they could grow up. Their comment was a pleasant, sweet-tasting surprise to me and another confirmation that God works all things for good.

December 4. *"The Spirit said to Philip, 'Go near and overtake this chariot'"* (Acts 8:29).

This is an example of the Spirit leading a believer and the believer immediately being obedient. We should not hesitate when God's will becomes known to us.

Sometimes during the night the name of a person, the name of a place, or a situation will come to me in a dream. This has been happening to me periodically for many years. At first, I ignored these images, believing that they were nothing more than random thoughts in my subconscious. Now I believe these images come to me from the Holy Spirit, prompting me to pray for someone in a specific place or situation. So now, every time this happens, I immediately pray for God to protect the person whom the Spirit has brought to mind, rebuking any possible harm that may befall them in their present circumstances.

Although I do not know if the people, places, and situations that come to me at night are real, I will nevertheless continue to pray. I will not question whether these images are really from the Holy Spirit or are just random dream-thoughts. Scripture tells us to pray for one another and to pray continuously. What happens next is up to God. So I will pray whenever I receive an image in my mind at night, and every time I do, a sense of peace and purpose fills me. I am at ease knowing that somebody, somewhere, might have actually benefited because I heeded God's call and intervened with a prayer.

> *The Spirit also helps in our weaknesses. For we do not know what we should pray for as we ought, but the Spirit Himself makes intercession for us with groanings which cannot be uttered.* (Romans 8:26)

Last night in my sleep, the name "Seymour" came to me in a dream. In that semiconscious world between sleep and wakefulness, I thought I remembered a town in Arizona named Seymour. Later that morning I searched the internet to see if the town of Seymour might actually exist. It did not. Perhaps Seymour was a person living in Arizona. Despite how bizarre this may sound to somebody else, faith is having confidence in something that one cannot see or, in worldly terms, understand. In faith, I asked God to protect this person named Seymour in Arizona, a total stranger to me.

The incident reminded me again of all the people God had surrounded me with, including medical experts, to offer encouragement and uphold me in prayer—all the people He had called to be my angels preventing me from "striking my foot against a stone" (see Psalm 91). Even if these people did not realize that God had called them to be in my life at this time, I knew it. I knew His presence through them, and the experience was truly humbling. Perhaps I was to be an unseen, praying angel for a stranger named Seymour. Only God knows for sure.

December 5. Despite feeling exhausted, I was up in time to attend an early strategic business meeting at my company. How easy it would have been to stay in bed, yet my battle with cancer was not about me. It was about God and my responsibility to care for His flock, those whom God had placed in my care through my company.

That night I spoke to a small group of MBA students at a local college. Again, it would have been easy to postpone my talk until after I had recovered, yet I was committed to being God's shepherd and servant, to do what I believed was His will.

Be shepherds of God's flock that is under your care, watching over them—not because you must, but because you are willing, as God wants you to be;... eager to serve. (1 Peter 5:2 NIV)

December 6. This morning I reflected on the speech I gave last night to the MBA students. Only three students attended the class, yet if I influenced only one of them, the effort was worthwhile.

My topic had been ethics. I emphasized that we must first have a set of personal principles and values in order to live our lives; then, by example we can positively influence those around us. I explained how, eventually, those personal principles and values could also be foundational to our corporate values. If a conflict occurs between one's personal and corporate values, it may become necessary to move on because no situation should force us to compromise our personal principles and values. Needless to say, the source of my personal principles and values was the Bible.

I am often humbled that people see how I'm handling my trial, and that they see in me confidence and peace. I want them to know that my peace is the Lord's doing, not mine, that I am only trying to walk hand-in-hand with Him along this journey.

Be anxious for nothing, but in everything by prayer and supplication, with thanksgiving, let your requests be made known to God; and the peace of God, which surpasses all understanding, will guard your hearts and minds through Christ Jesus. (Philippians 4:6–7)

I thank God for this peace, and I pray that it will cover me throughout my life. This peace is a true blessing, and a fulfilled promise of God:

[Jesus speaking] *"Peace I leave with you, My peace I give to you; not as the world gives do I give to you. Let not your heart be troubled, neither let it be afraid."* (John 14:27)

December 7. Over the last two days I have attended several strategic business meetings at my company. I have always felt it is important to set an example, both in appearance and manner, of what a good leader should be. What I have noticed is that people look for confidence in their leader, and a leader exudes this confidence by what he or she says and does. Confidence in a leader gives confidence and hope to the flock. Since people read the body language of a leader, I try to always be "on" at my company. Given my circumstances at this time, this has become more important to me than ever before.

Be of good courage, and let us be strong for our people. (1 Chronicles 19:13)

Throughout the years, I have visited many people in the hospital, at their homes, at their weddings, and at the funerals of their loved ones. During many of those occasions, I have shared words of encouragement, especially with those who have cancer.

Although I did not feel convicted to talk with everyone about my journey, I also did not want anybody to speculate or worry about my health. Since I usually felt great, I thought I should act so.

All too often, worry can consume us. This is a normal and worldly reaction. Only by God's grace and mercy can we have a sense of peace. We must share this peace with others.

It was the Christmas season, the time of year God gave us peace through the birth of His Son, Jesus Christ. Christmas is the time we should celebrate this great gift from our heavenly Father. I felt I must share the peace God had given me with others.

December 8. Last night the Holy Spirit gave me another name in a dream. At first I was frightened my dream indicated that it was the name of a missing person, and it was also the name of my youngest son. Moments later, awakened, I knew the missing person was a younger child and not my son. Immediately I got up and prayed that God would protect the missing child.

This next morning my daily devotion was:

If anyone is a hearer of the word and not a doer, he is like a man observing his natural face in a mirror; for he observes himself, goes away, and immediately forgets what kind of man he was. But he who looks into the perfect law of liberty and continues in it, and is not a forgetful hearer but a doer of the work, this one will be blessed in what he does. (James 1:23–25)

In essence, this Bible passage means we should do what the Word of God says, in a spirit of obedience and faith, and by doing so He will bless us. I believed in my heart that God was using me as an intercessor for others and as an example to encourage others in being followers of Jesus Christ. I felt blessed beyond words.

Your word is a lamp to my feet and a light to my path. (Psalm 119:105)

Commit your way to the Lord, trust also in Him, and He shall bring it to pass. He shall bring forth your righteousness as the light, and your justice as the noonday. (Psalm 37:5–6)

Throughout this period, I have been led to be a light of encouragement irrespective of any anxiety or doubt within me. The irony of it is that I do not have time to worry about myself. I am serving others. It is a true blessing while it gives me deep joy.

12.
THE LIGHT OF CHRIST

Let your light so shine before men, that they may see your good works and glorify your Father in heaven.

Matthew 5:16

As the day of my surgery drew closer, so did the completion of my vitamin treatments. The objective of the vitamin was to reduce my cancer burden. I would need another body scan to determine whether surgery was still necessary or, with the reduction of the cancer burden, if I could postpone the surgery.

It was at that point that I started to feel a little anxious.

What if the cancer's gotten worse instead of better? I thought. *Maybe I shouldn't bother with the scan and just go ahead with the surgery.*

I think I was looking for excuses not to get the scan in case it would reveal bad news.

So I arrived at the infusion clinic prepared with an excuse as to why I should not have another scan. My excuse, however, was not a part of God's plan for me, as I quickly learned the moment I saw Dr. Baker.

Bubbling with excitement, she smiled at me and said, "This morning I attended the university faculty Bible study!" Her excitement escalated. "And you'll never believe who was there!"

My excitement rose to match Dr. Baker's the moment I heard her say, "It was Dr. Swanson in radiology, the doctor who developed the scan protocol."

Instantly we both knew what that meant. Dr. Swanson was a fellow believer, and neither Dr. Baker nor I had known. But God knew, and He was the one who had brought the three of us together.

At that moment, I again knew that God was in control and that I must not fret. I would do whatever Drs. Baker and Swanson decided, because they were both God's servants prepared by Him to do His will for me. Both were among the army of angels God had placed all around me!

In retrospect, I realize that, in my anxious moments, I was attempting to manipulate or control the path God had set for me. I needed to remember the scriptural command:

Cast all [my] anxiety on Him because He cares for [me]. (1 Peter 5:7)

What a liberating fact of Scripture—that *God actually invites us to give our worries to Him*. As I did so, God replaced my anxiety with His peace and joy. I would continue to trust Him to heal me, even if my pathway included more scans or surgery.

I also believed anew that God had called Dr. Baker to help me and that the vitamin infusion protocol was a key part of my journey to healing, regardless of whether I would also need surgery. I *had* to relax, get the scan, and complete the vitamin protocol—with no expectations as to what I wanted, but for God's purpose and glory.

That evening Martha and I attended a Christmas party. While there we came across Sarah, a dear friend who was going through a rough time personally. As Sarah was bringing us up to date, I knew she needed words of encouragement.

Suddenly she stopped and asked me, "How are *you* doing?" I took the opportunity to share Philippians 4:6–7 with her:

Be anxious for nothing, but in everything by prayer and supplication, with thanksgiving, let your requests be made known to God; and the peace of God, which surpasses all understanding, will guard your hearts and minds through Christ Jesus.

I told Sarah about the peace I had, a peace that I could not explain, a peace that God had given me. I told her that God could give her that same peace. She smiled at us and said, "I'm so grateful that the two of you stopped by to talk with me. I know it was not by chance."

Martha and I both felt God had placed us in that place at that time to share His love with someone in need.

December 9. A dear friend of Martha's called and told her, "I've been praying for your husband."

SURROUNDED BY ANGELS

I had many people praying for me. Some I knew and some I did not know. But God knew all of them, and He was listening to every one of their prayers. I trusted God, knowing He had a specific purpose for me.

Dr. Charles Stanley's daily devotion for today included the following thoughts:

If God chooses us for a task, He will give us all the strength and wisdom we need to complete that task. All we need is a willing and obedient spirit.

Moses said to God, "Who am I that I should go to Pharaoh, and that I should bring the children of Israel out of Egypt?" So He [God] said, "I will certainly be with you." (Exodus 3:11–12)

[Gideon] said to Him, "O my Lord, how can I save Israel? Indeed my clan is the weakest in Manasseh, and I am the least in my father's house." And the Lord said to him, "Surely I will be with you." (Judges 6:15–16)

Neither Moses nor Gideon would have expected God to choose them for the purposes He had. I believed God had chosen me, too, for a purpose.

Throughout my life, I had always hoped I would be at the pinnacle of health. I exercised regularly. I kept a strict diet. I maintained a healthy weight. I also had regular checkups. Yet now I had cancer. I was the one person most people, including myself, never expected to become ill.

A key part of the battle, however, is that I put my trust in God and let go, to be His instrument to bring love, joy, and peace to others. I believed in God's promises. I believed He would be with me just as He had promised to be with Moses and Gideon. There have been so many instances, big and small, where I have already felt, heard, and seen God's presence through those around me.

In Dr. Charles Stanley's devotion today, he stated that the light of Jesus Christ in us allows Him to shine where we model His ways in our conversation, our conduct, and our character ... a righteous lifestyle gets attention ... others who see our light will want it for themselves ... our light will lead people to Jesus.

In the beginning was the Word, and the Word was with God, and the Word was God. He was in the beginning with God. All things were made through Him, and without Him nothing was made that was made. In Him was life, and the life was the light of men. And the light shines in the darkness, and the darkness did not comprehend it. (John 1:1–5)

Jesus spoke to them again, saying, "I am the light of the world. He who follows Me shall not walk in darkness, but have the light of life." (John 8:12)

[Jesus speaking] *"You are the light of the world. A city that is set on a hill cannot be hidden."* (Matthew 5:14)

Yesterday I received a beautiful email message from a good friend:

Ted: I have had you and your wife on my mind, and I wanted you to know how much I appreciate your friendship. One year ago, I was going through a life-altering experience, and I came out a better person (still need improvement). I know you and your wife helped me with your prayers. Additionally, over the last several years, I have been privileged to observe your lifestyle. The way you interact with your family and friends is a lesson for us all. Just look at your boys, great chips off the old block. They will do great things. I am not sure what moved me to tell you this today. It never hurts to let someone know they are loved.

I replied:

What a blessing to read your email. It was very special from a special person. Fast forward this year, and I am embarking on a life-changing event also. We can swap advice. I cannot explain it in human terms, but the peace of God does exist. I never expected to understand it, let alone feel it, so I feel really blessed. It is all part of a big plan. Meeting you and forming a new company is part of this plan. While I never wanted to be in this situation, I also have faith that it will be to God's glory. Your prayers are needed to help me in this journey of healing. Thanks for being my friend.

Many times, without my even realizing it, the Lord has used my smile to shine His light on others. People have told me, "Your smile reflects the Holy Spirit within you."

I have commented, "I do it unconsciously."

Sharing my testimony and drawing others to Him, through word and deed, is for the glory of God. The Lord has indeed shined His face on me and has given me grace and peace. I will continue try to radiate His peace to others around me.

13.
MINISTERING ANGELS

*He shall give His angels charge over you,
to keep you in all your ways.*

Psalm 91:11

December 10. Dr. David Morehouser is one of America's foremost complementary medicine practitioners and is host of a nationally syndicated radio program.

Yesterday I called Dr. Morehouser at his office. I wanted to ask him about an herb that may promote healthy cell growth. Although I was not a patient of his, the woman who answered the phone graciously offered to call the doctor at his home and ask him my question. Within the hour, she called me back with a helpful answer.

I complimented her on her compassion and kindness. "I understand your situation," she said, "and I hope I was able to help you."

I was a total stranger to this woman, yet she graciously helped me. She did not know who I was, yet she called the doctor at home for me, even though I was not his patient. Who was I to call such a well-known doctor out of the blue and expect to receive an answer? Again, I was humbled to experience God's grace through others.

December 11. Although I was feeling tired, I attended a meeting of Christian business leaders. Afterward one of the members approached me.

"May I pray for you?" he asked.

"I'd be honored," I told him, and we retreated to a corner where he prayed with me for God's strength, healing, and peace.

When we finished, he said, "You're always available to pray for others. You prayed for me when I was sick. I just wanted to return the blessing."

It was a wonderful act of faith, which I deeply appreciated. God was continuing to surround me with people who wanted to help me.

The beat goes on! It is always special to feel the presence of God's love through others.

December 12. Again, God led me to another resource for help.

I contacted the office of another prominent doctor by email and by phone, leaving a voicemail message. God was again faithful. Within the hour I received a response to the email message I had sent, and at the end of the day I received a phone call from an unknown number. That was amazing! The doctor actually called me and asked, "Do you need any more information?" He was supportive and encouraging, confirming that the path I had chosen was the right path to take. I would be in great hands with my surgeon and everything would be fine.

Again, another stranger had connected with me in a time of need. Whether the doctor realized it or not, he was another angel God had commanded to watch over me. Thank You, Lord!

My friend Rich felt led by the Spirit to pray for me. God knew I would be concerned about prayer support, so He sent one of His faithful servants to pray for me before I had a chance to doubt. In addition to Rich, the father of another friend also wanted to pray for me before my surgery—another example of how God, through them, was demonstrating His love and care.

14.
THE NEXT STEP OF FAITH

We walk by faith, not by sight.
2 Corinthians 5:7

December 13. It is all about God's will and timing. For me it was time to have this specific trial. God knew I was ready for the next step of faith; that I would wait on Him for direction, guidance, and confirmation; that my heart and mind would know when He was present; that then and only then would I act on His will.

Humble yourselves under the mighty hand of God, that He may exalt you in due time. (1 Peter 5:6)

December 14. By serving others, we serve God.

"If anyone serves Me, let him follow Me; and where I am, there My servant will be also. If anyone serves Me, him My Father will honor." (John 12:26)

[Jesus speaking] *"The King will answer and say to them, 'Assuredly, I say to you, inasmuch as you did it to one of the least of these My brethren, you did it to Me.'"* (Matthew 25:40)

[Jesus speaking] *"His lord said to him, 'Well done, good and faithful servant; you were faithful over a few things, I will make you ruler over many things. Enter into the joy of your lord.'"* (Matthew 25:21)

Theodore Mistra

Throughout my study of faith in the workplace, I try to seek His will and serve Him by serving the needs of others. When asked what I would like on my epitaph I say, "Well done, good and faithful shepherd."

From my journal:

Tomorrow I will undergo another scan to determine if I will need surgery. People all around me have been praying that surgery will not be necessary. My hope is still that I won't need surgery, but my trust is in the Lord my God. Whatever the outcome, I am at peace.

Last night God put in my mind that being His servant is a key building block in learning unconditional submission to His will in our walk of faith. "Well done, good and faithful servant" is the accolade I want to hear from God. He impressed me that before one can be a shepherd, he or she must first be a servant. While I have lived my life as a servant, a leader, and a shepherd, I can now truly understand the significance of being His servant.

My peace along this journey is the act, whether conscious or unconscious, of complete submission to God, of knowing deep down in my soul and heart that He works all things together for good for those who love Him and are called according to His purpose. A servant does not disobey his master. A servant submits to his master's will without second-guessing or doubt, totally relying on the wisdom of the master. It is extremely hard to understand this revelation because we think in human terms. We think about "evil" masters with "evil" intentions. But God is good and merciful. I do not question why I have cancer. Something inside me checked any wayward thoughts—the Holy Spirit, who is far more powerful than my human inclinations and who has overwhelmed any evil thoughts in me. The Holy Spirit is a gift from God, the Helper and Comforter Jesus Christ promised to every believer.

The Holy Spirit, Jesus said, will teach us many things, and bring to remembrance things we have learned, heard, or seen in Christ Jesus. I can indeed attest that the Helper, the Holy Spirit, is in us who believe in Jesus Christ as our Lord and Savior—and that the more deeply and powerfully the Holy Spirit reveals Himself to us, the more He can guide and protect us from evil.

15.
BEYOND FEAR

*I sought the L*ORD*, and He heard me,
and delivered me from all my fears.*

Psalm 34:4

December 17. Although we did not yet have the results of the latest scan, after praying about God's will and ultimate pathway to healing, Martha and I decided that I would proceed with the surgery. I was at peace with my decision, which I believed was God's will for my healing.

However, I could sense areas of anxiety in the periphery of my mind. They were faint, and I intended to keep them faint by counting on my joy, perseverance, character, hope, and love of God.

To show my appreciation to all those "angels" who had encouraged me along the way, I had the words to the song "On Eagle's Wings" printed on a card that I could give as a gift, attached with a personal note of thanks.

Without consciously volunteering to have cancer for the glory of God, I knew intuitively that I was chosen by Him for this journey. God had transformed my heart. Better me than others dear to me who might not have the depth and breadth of faith nor the peace of Him who dwells in me. This is a gift from God planted in me, which I could not understand except by facing the trial and trusting the Comforter to come alive and give me strength.

Before Martha and I flew to the Mayo Clinic, a friend prayed over me. As part of his prayer, he read Psalm 91:14–15:

[God speaking] *He has set his love upon Me, therefore I will deliver him; I will set him on high, because he has known My name. He shall call upon Me, and I will answer him; I will be with him in trouble; I will deliver him and honor him.*

This was a sincere expression of my friend's faith in God to deliver me from the cancer. I deeply appreciated his prayer and his faith.

After we arrived in Minnesota and checked into a hotel near the Mayo Clinic, we enjoyed a relaxing dinner at the hotel. I shared with Martha that I had asked God to take away my fear and, as a maturing Christian, to help me understand what He was leading me through. This was something I had also asked God prior to my cancer.

After dinner, we strolled through some of the subways, tunnels, and skyways of the Mayo Clinic. Rochester was beautiful, with the ground blanketed in snow, and the night was peaceful with so few people out.

When we returned to our hotel, my friend Rich had left a message for me to call him. When I returned his call, he prayed with me over the phone. "We ask for glory, healing, and long life that will be a testimony to You, Lord," Rich prayed. "Surround Ted with Your angels to protect him. I pray for the Holy Spirit to rule in Ted's life, and that everything to be done is guided by You."

What a blessing to be surrounded by friends like Rich ... friends who were lifting me up in prayer and encouraging and helping at each step along my journey. That evening I wrote in my journal:

> I can now say I do not fear death. I am in His hands completely, obedient to His will. I could glorify God in whatever manner He chooses to use me. I believe I have borne much fruit, and that I could bear even more fruit in the future—that my life is just beginning a new journey that will be more fruitful than my first sixty years. But God may decide otherwise, and who am I to question Him? I am His servant.

SURROUNDED BY ANGELS

December 18. I heard back from the hospital that my scan showed significant improvement. Seemingly, the vitamin treatments were successful in reducing the cancer load. Surgery, however, was still an instrumental part of my journey to healing, a part I was still at peace with.

I prayed for that peace to continue. I prayed for the Holy Spirit to be present in the operating room during my surgery, and that the surgeon's hands, Dr. Peterson's hands, would be one with the hands of God. I must admit, though, that I wasn't as concerned about the actual surgery as I was about the requisite urethra catheterization. While I knew that the catheter would only be temporary, I prayed that it would not be too bothersome.

Rich and his wife called again, and this time they both prayed. "Lord, we are in awe of what You have done in Ted's heart and spirit, getting him ready for surgery; and also what You have done for his family and for his business," Rich prayed.

"Rest. Peace. Ted is in Your hands, Lord," his wife joined in. "Lord, we believe the prostate problem will be taken care of. We pray for long life in the next season, that all the cancer cells will be taken out.

"Lift Ted up. May he see angels guiding the steps of the people in the operating room. Amen."

December 19. Although I never felt the need to tell everyone about my battle with cancer, I was at peace about the extent of sharing I had done. The numerous phone calls and email messages I received prior to my surgery from family and friends, as well as the countless prayers offered by so many, were of immeasurable comfort to me.

I knew I was in God's hands.

As Martha and I walked through the subway beneath the Mayo Clinic campus to the Rochester Methodist Hospital, I began to feel trepidation. For a brief moment I wanted to flee, but I knew I must fulfill this part of the journey, which I knew would play a major part in my healing.

I asked God, "When will I see the angels?"

It was 5:45 A.M. when we arrived at the admissions desk. The area was crowded with others who were also waiting for surgery. After checking in, we sat in a couple of chairs outside the entrance to the lobby. Too nervous to sit still, though, I stood and began looking around.

When I heard my name called, I knew I could no longer turn back.

As we proceeded, something prompted me to stop and look inside a display case. Behind the glass was a collection of beautiful ceramic and glass angels. I was stunned. As I stood there, captivated by those beautiful angels, God assured me that He would be present every step of the way, that I would feel His presence whenever there came a need. This was, indeed, God's answer to my nervous question. He had shown me the angels.

As we continued toward surgery, God continued to show me His presence along the way. We passed a beautiful stained-glass mural made up of several panels. Two of the panels caught my attention immediately. The first panel depicted a crown and a shepherd's staff. On the second panel was a white dove, the symbol of the Holy Spirit. Further along we passed a cross hanging on the wall, and in my dressing room was a Bible. I knew I was not alone: God was indeed with me. Although I still felt a few twinges of nervousness, God's love and presence—symbolized by the wonderful artwork that had ministered to me along the way—triumphed and overwhelmed the nerves. I was strengthened by His supernatural strength and peace.

After I'd dressed in a hospital gown, a nurse escorted me to the prep room. Despite all the hustle and bustle around me, I never felt alone or like a number. The compassion from all the staff permeated the hospital culture.

The anesthesiologist was making his way around the prep room checking everybody's name. He was a big, jolly sort of man who walked with intensity and purpose. As soon as he checked my name, he looked up at me.

"Rock-Chalk-Jayhawk!" he exclaimed with a huge grin.

For over a hundred years the Rock Chalk chant has been the battle cry of the Kansas University fans. Martha and I are big KU fans—especially Martha. My anesthesiologist, I would learn, had graduated from the KU medical school!

Can you imagine my feeling of joy and excitement? Here, in the midst of one of the largest surgical centers in the world, a doctor sang out "Rock Chalk Jayhawk." If I had been feeling any lingering fear, it would have been crushed completely. Instead, the doctor and I were laughing and joking about the Jayhawks basketball team just minutes before my surgery.

We actually talked more about KU than about my surgery. I didn't mind! Our conversation made me feel that my anesthesiologist really cared about me—not just as a patient, but as a person. He helped me feel more at ease, knowing that God had connected me with yet another of His angels.

They wheeled me into the operating room, where another surprise awaited me. As my anesthesiologist, my new friend, prepared to put me under, he led the entire surgical staff in singing the Jayhawks Fight Song. So even as I was beginning to fade, God brought me not only this one angel, but also a whole choir of singing angels.

Within moments I was out, surrounded by His angels. How sweet I felt!

16.
BY GOD'S GRACE

*Sin shall not have dominion over you,
for you are not under law but under grace.*

Romans 6:14

Six hours later, I opened my eyes in the recovery room and immediately saw a cross hanging on the wall. God also comforted me through the caring staff that was attending to my every need.

A bit later, as the nurse wheeled me into my room, I saw a painting of Jesus on the wall. It was as if God was welcoming me back from surgery! Excited about the picture, I asked the nurse, "What do others think about it?"

"We have that picture in many of the hospital rooms," she replied. "If it makes you feel uncomfortable, I'll remove it."

"What do you think of it?" I asked her.

"I'm a Christian," she said, "so I personally love it."

"Me, too," I agreed. "I'm a Christian too, and I love having a picture of Jesus in my room. Will you tell me a little about yourself?"

The nurse took the time to share openly about her Christian home life as a child. She had grown up with four sisters and had attended a Christian college. The connection between the two of us was immediate—and very comforting. She was another angel whom God had provided along my journey.

I told her, "You're one of the angels God promised me."

She beamed.

"In Psalm 91 God promises to give His angels charge over us."

Before she left, I reminded her to read the ninety-first Psalm.

She was finishing her shift, so she asked, "Would you read it to me?"

I obliged. Happily. There I was, just a few hours out of prostate surgery, reading Psalm 91 with another of God's children:

He who dwells in the secret place of the Most High shall abide under the shadow of the Almighty. I will say of the Lord, "He is my refuge and my fortress; My God, in Him I will trust."

Surely He shall deliver you from the snare of the fowler and from the perilous pestilence. He shall cover you with His feathers, and under His wings you shall take refuge; His truth shall be your shield and buckler. You shall not be afraid of the terror by night, nor of the arrow that flies by day, nor of the pestilence that walks in darkness, nor of the destruction that lays waste at noonday.

A thousand may fall at your side, and ten thousand at your right hand; but it shall not come near you. Only with your eyes shall you look, and see the reward of the wicked.

Because you have made the Lord, who is my refuge, even the Most High, your dwelling place, no evil shall befall you, nor shall any plague come near your dwelling; for He shall give His angels charge over you, to keep you in all your ways. In their hands they shall bear you up, lest you dash your foot against a stone. You shall tread upon the lion and the cobra, the young lion and the serpent you shall trample underfoot.

"Because he has set his love upon Me, therefore I will deliver him; I will set him on high, because he has known My name. He shall call upon Me, and I will answer him; I will be with him in trouble; I will deliver him and honor him. With long life I will satisfy him, and show him My salvation."

When I finished reading, I could see that Psalm 91 had touched her. Before she left my room, we clasped hands, and the moment that passed between us was something special. During my stay in the hospital, this nurse—another angel—visited me several more times, and each time we talked about our faith.

Later the assisting surgeon visited me to discuss the specifics of my surgery. I shared with him how comfortable I was having an angel for one of my nurses. Without hesitating he said, "I'm also a believer." I did not know this before he said it, but God knew.

God had guided this man's assisting hands during my surgery, and I never had a reason for concern. God is faithful!

That evening my surgeon, Dr. Peterson, paid me a visit. From his report he read:

- success story,
- operation went nicely,
- negative margins,

- nice reading from pathology,
- cancer all contained,
- operation took an extra hour, but I wanted to be careful,
- took great care of your nerves,
- expect an excellent outcome.

The surgery was a success! Praise the Lord! He had surrounded me with angels, and He had guided the surgical team.

17.
CROSSED PATHS

Do not forget to do good and to share, for with such sacrifices God is well pleased.

Hebrews 13:16

December 20. Early in the day I felt a need to reach out to the assistant surgeon. When he visited with me again, I encouraged him to read the Bible and to continue using his gift from God to help others. I shared Jeremiah 33:3 with him, a Bible passage that my friend Rich had shared with me for encouragement.

> *"Call to Me, and I will answer you, and show you great and mighty things, which you do not know."* (Jeremiah 33:3)

As we spent more time together, I learned that he had interviewed for a urology residency elsewhere but chose to practice at the Mayo Clinic in Rochester, Minnesota, because he felt the Mayo program was best for him.

Later that day the nurse came to give me a blood transfusion. She mentioned that her sister was at the same medical center where Dr. Baker practiced.

Being surrounded by familiar things brought more comfort. It is another example how God blesses us through others, how He can carry out His will through them. Whether they know it or not, God knows it, and I know it.

That evening a group of volunteers sang Christmas carols throughout the hospital. When the carolers reached my floor, Martha and I stopped talking and listened as the singers made their rounds. To hear the words and the melodies of the traditional carols—the carols that glorify the birth of Jesus Christ—warmed our hearts.

I felt blessed to be in a hospital that welcomed Christ in its midst. While I was at the Mayo Clinic, I saw patients from all cultures around the world and watched the doctors and nurses giving loving care to every one of them, as Christ would have them do.

When the carolers reached my room, they stopped and sang, of all songs, "Hark! The Herald Angels Sing."

That night God had sent a whole chorus of angels to warm my heart.

December 21. I now had an eighty-four-year-old man as a roommate. He was as feisty as could be, yet funny and friendly. We got along well. Just before the hospital released him, he said, "I hope the doctor gives me good news, because I could use it." He had already lost two wives and two children.

"I'll pray for you," I said.

He asked, "Are you a Christian?"

"I am." We prayed together and said our goodbyes.

Later that day I, too, checked out of the hospital and moved into the hotel.

December 22. On this day I hit bottom. I was no exception to what typically happens in the days following surgery: pain, exhaustion, discouragement. As the swelling peaked and the pain-killing drugs wore off, the pain became unbearable. I prayed for relief but knew I would have to endure the next couple of days. I knew I had to focus on my blessings. It was much easier to dwell on the pain and discomfort, but I had to find and focus on the blessings in the midst of it all.

I tried to keep my mind on the fact that God was healing me and the cancer was gone.

December 23 was a new day, a new beginning. God intervened. The painful spasms and the related anxiety I had felt yesterday were much more tolerable today. Martha and I rested in our hotel room and prayed. We prayed that God would heal me quickly from the surgery. The two drainage cups were a nuisance, so we prayed that I would not need them much longer and that tomorrow the doctor would remove them before we headed home.

SURROUNDED BY ANGELS

Martha and I also reflected on the personal attention that the three concierges at the hotel gave us during our stay. As a token of our appreciation, we gave each of them one of the cards I had printed up with the song "On Eagle's Wings." On each card, I wrote: "You were my angel."

December 24. God is good! This morning, upon awakening, I felt better than I did yesterday. The drainage cups were clear, and when I visited the doctor, he removed them. God had answered our prayers.

The doctor—the assistant surgeon and fellow believer—told me, "I will be on call throughout Christmas. If you need anything, please call me."

I said I didn't want to bother him, but he insisted he was there to help me at any time. What a blessing that turned out to be. It gave me a complete sense of peace, and I knew immediately that God understood the apprehension I was feeling, and He had orchestrated it all.

I shared my conviction with the doctor and said a little prayer for him.

"How nice it is to help another believer," he said.

For some reason, I was distracted while leaving the hospital. When we entered the elevator to go down to the lobby, Martha had to grab my attention to show me that two nuns were sharing the elevator with us. They were from the nursing staff at St. Mary's hospital, another Mayo affiliate hospital in Rochester. During my previous visits, I had never seen the nursing sisters at the main clinic, only at St. Mary's.

When I looked their way, they smiled and wished us a Merry Christmas. Tears filled my eyes when I realized that God had never once forsaken me during my trial. Even now, He provided two angels to escort me out of the hospital. The experience was humbling, and I am eternally grateful to our Father in heaven.

December 25. Christmas morning, I reflected on all the people who had ministered to me—all the angels God had given charge over me as promised in Psalm 91. I'm sure I missed some, but those who came to mind included:

- the surgical team of doctors that removed my cancer,
- the nurses who cared for me,

- the people at the hotel who accommodated me,
- the volunteers who sang Christmas songs glorifying God to me,
- the two nuns in the elevator who gave me one last reminder of God's love for me,
- everyone who supported, encouraged, and prayed for me,
- everyone who spoke a kind word or smiled for me, and
- everyone who had created a piece of artwork that touched my heart or reminded me of God's promises.

God had given the gift of mercy to all those people and sent them my way to minister to me and my needs—physical, spiritual, and emotional—during my journey toward healing.

In our home, we have two watercolor paintings in our sunroom. Both are of angels. While I was recuperating in the sunroom, I studied the paintings and realized that, until now, I had never fully appreciated the promises and the presence of God.

When we ask, seek, and knock, God will answer our prayers, and we will find comfort in His presence. God will never leave us, nor will He ever forsake us.

> [Jesus speaking] *"I say to you, ask, and it will be given to you; seek, and you will find; knock, and it will be opened to you."* (Luke 11:9)

18.
THIS JOURNEY ENDS

These things I have spoken to you, that in Me you may have peace.
In the world you will have tribulation; but be of good cheer,
I have overcome the world.

John 16:33

December 26. I keep a prayer list of everything I ask God for, checking off each prayer as He answers it.

When I learned I had prostate cancer, I wrote a prayer request, number nine in my prayer journal. The prayer was that "I would be healed of prostate cancer, be a witness to those who care for me and to have no fear on the journey." Today I checked off prayer number nine.

When my surgeon, Dr. Peterson, had visited me in the hospital, he spoke with complete confidence. He had said, "You can consider yourself cured of prostate cancer." I had never doubted the outcome. I had trusted God wholeheartedly for healing.

Not for a moment had I feared my cancer, my outcome, or my future. From the start, I had placed my trust in God and experienced His peace. The moments of fear I had felt prior to surgery had quickly dissipated when God revealed His presence through all the signs along my path. He ministered peace through all the kind, caring people he had placed around me. I knew God had been right there among the surgical team during my surgery.

Yes, God had answered prayer number nine.

I recalled times at Mayo Clinic when God had called me to witness to others.

I thought of

- the nurse to whom I had read Psalm 91,
- the assistant surgeon whom I had encouraged to read the Bible and to continue using his gift from God to help others, and
- my eighty-four-year-old roommate who had needed somebody to pray for him.

Even during this, the toughest part of my healing journey, God had used me to bless others for His glory.

For the last two days I have been bothered with nausea, cramping, and a lack of appetite—symptoms caused by an allergy to some dairy products I unintentionally ingested. In the past, those symptoms would have lasted only a few hours. While the symptoms made me miserable, I knew they would pass. They were minor compared to God's plan.

This is the day the Lord *has made; we will rejoice and be glad in it.* (Psalm 118:24)

I must now go on with my life with no distractions. I must focus on glorifying God.

December 27. I felt better, yet I took it much easier than anticipated. I reflected on Psalm 118:24, which God had put on my heart again that morning: "This is the day the Lord has made; we will rejoice and be glad in it." So I persevered and truly enjoyed the day recovering from the setback.

December 28. Recovered from my food allergy, I felt complete again, and once more God called me to be a witness. I told our housekeeper about the ceramic and glass angels I had seen in the display window at the hospital prior to my surgery. I said to her, "God is everywhere, but it is up to us to ask, seek, and knock. Because God is faithful and just, He will respond to us, but if we are not looking, we will miss the encounter."

"I needed that type of encouragement today," she said with a smile.

SURROUNDED BY ANGELS

Even inside my own home, someone had needed to hear encouraging words. It would have been so easy to sit there thinking only of myself. But God had prompted me to bear witness and share my experience with someone who needed to hear.

In my journal I wrote:

I must take every opportunity to witness to everybody who is ready and open,
no matter what my circumstances are or where I may be.

December 30. Today Martha and I visited our farm in the country. It was cold, but the bright sunshine and blue skies were magnificent.

When I entered our barn to leave a check for our farm helper, I noticed that she had left a Christmas gift for us. It was a ceramic angel, and the angel was holding the baby Jesus. She had not known about my trial, nor was she aware of the special significance that angels had in my recent life, yet something had prompted her to give us that particular gift for Christmas.

I now had a beautiful ceramic angel of my own. God's presence in our barn was another sign that He is everywhere in our lives.

Tomorrow is the last day of the year. Looking forward to the new year is exciting!

19.
THE NEW THING

I will go to the altar of God,
to God my exceeding joy;
and on the harp I will praise You,
O God, my God.

Psalm 43:4

December 31. At 4:00 A.M. a dream roused me from my sleep and prompted me to read Isaiah 49. I got out of bed, sat at my desk, and opened my Bible. The chapter was a command from God, epitomized by verses 3 and 8.

> *You are MY servant, O Israel,*
> *In whom I will be glorified* (verse 3, emphasis added).

> *I will preserve you and give you*
> *as a covenant to the people* (verse 8).

I had read Isaiah 49 back in September during one of my daily studies. At that time, God was already preparing me, placing in my heart that He was choosing me for something special, that I was to be His servant, that through my obedience He would bless me and my children. I sensed back then that God was calling me to begin a new and more powerful journey, yet I had no idea what that journey would be.

Several weeks later when I learned that I had cancer, God's words had already permeated my heart, soul, and mind. His peace had strengthened me from the start. But I did not fully realize it at the time. I just believed the promise.

Shortly after my journey began, God also had led my friend Rich and another friend of mine to share Isaiah 49 with me. Both confirmed my work for God, that He had called me to bear witness to glorify Him. Now, once again on December 31, God was guiding me back to Isaiah 49. He was leading me back so I would not forget my calling. It was very humbling.

Today marks the end of one journey and the beginning of a new one. My new journey will be to glorify God by bearing much fruit. I am never to look back or dwell on the cancer. From this day forward, I am to draw inspiration from God's abundance of grace and mercy to me, and will be an encouragement to others by sharing my journey and blessings with them.

Indeed, God does reward those who obey Him.

I called the doctor's office and left a voicemail message. In less than a minute, the nurse returned my call and scheduled an appointment for an x-ray to determine when my catheter could be removed.

I knew she could not have listened to my message and returned my call in less than a minute. Instead, the receptionist had immediately listened and relayed my message to the nurse, giving her my number. Only God could have orchestrated this. The nurse and the receptionist, both strangers to me, were angels of God.

January 1. Henry T. Blackaby[10] is the founder and president emeritus of Blackaby Ministries International, an organization built to help people experience God. His devotion today was from Isaiah.

> *Behold, I will do a* NEW THING,
> *Now it shall spring forth;*
> *Shall you not know it?*
> *I will even make a road in the wilderness*
> *And rivers in the desert.* (Isaiah 43:19, emphasis added).

---

10 Actual name.

This has always been a special and meaningful verse for me. In the past, when faced with difficulties at my company and with my children, I had meditated on this verse countless times. Each time, God had replaced despair with joy. Each time God had led, prompted, and guided me through the rivers, woods, and desert to victory.

I wrote in my journal:

> I must always trust God, seek His will, be patient, and obey Him. Once God shows me the way, it is up to me to take the first step and to follow Him, even if I cannot yet see the finish line.

January 2. My catheter was removed one week early.

As I begin my new journey, I wait for the Holy Spirit to prompt me and guide me. I pray that I will be obedient to the Word of God. It is not about me. It is about God in me, working through me in my words and my actions.

My helper is the Holy Spirit whom the Father has given to all His children who trust in Him. The Spirit within will teach me many things, guiding me along each step of this new journey.

January 3. My cancer is gone! I now eagerly wait for the Lord to show me His will for the future. I am excited about the "new thing" God is preparing for me.

20.
WHEN I CALL

*You shall call, and the Lord will answer;
you shall cry, and He will say, "Here I am."*

Isaiah 58:9

During my journey, God's presence and love for me was obvious and pervasive in everything I saw and did.

It has now been over fifteen years since I was diagnosed with prostate cancer; life continued then, still continues today, and I believe will continue as long as God so wills it. As we have heard in many sermons and in that wonderful old song, "God is not finished with me yet."

During this period my life continued to have its trials and tribulations, but God continued to be gracious to me, with blessings that flowed like "rivers of living waters." His presence through His Holy Spirit in me has been a constant companion. And if I look closely and listen carefully to the people around me, I continue to hear the words they speak and share with me, words God wants them to speak and share with me. Whether they realize it or not, God is using them as His messengers, and I consider them His angels.

To encourage your own life, whatever state you find yourself in, let me briefly share with you some of my life events that transpired over the past fifteen years since my near tragedy. They will encourage you to not just look at the moment of difficulty you are in but trust God to walk with you through that valley of death and on to the greatest moments yet to come. I am not only alive and well, but my three wonderful children each got married and blessed Martha and me with seven beautiful, healthy grandchildren. Martha and I have now been married over forty-four years. God is so gracious!

And the Lord's hints of my future being even greater than the period before I contacted my cancer have all come to pass. New business challenges and opportunities continued to be like a roller coaster, but through prayer, petition, and perseverance, they continue to allow me to overcome the "wiles of the world."

My prostate cancer never returned, and I continue to test negative. However, a few years later I had a second bout with a different cancer, but as before, God was faithful, and I trusted Him once again as He led me on a new pathway for healing. After an early diagnosis, which was once more a complete surprise to me, I underwent immediate treatment, and gratefully the second cancer rather quickly went into full remission and has remained negative ever since. And thankfully, I never had a single symptom or side effect from the treatment.

Looking back, I now consider the prostate cancer, in a sense, a trial by fire, and I am very thankful that through it all I learned to walk and grow to an even deeper faith. And just as the first time, I again was blessed with the love, joy, and peace of the army of angels who surrounded me throughout this second trial. What a blessing they were!

"Retired at last!" I thought. But no; instead, as Charles Stanley said in a popular sermon that is widely quoted, "God never intended us to retire but to refire our lives and continue to seek and do His will till the very end!" For me, while I did retire from the business world per se, I even more energetically reengaged in the world of ministry! I became very active in my local church, in a faith-based health care clinic, and at a Christian postsecondary school. In addition, I continue to give my personal testimony, while taking every opportunity to teach and write.

If you have read this testimony and been encouraged, thank you for letting me share my story with you, and please pass forward the blessing. I never forget that God is forever faithful and wants you to also be forever hopeful because He loves you. He is with you through His Holy Spirit in you now, and He promises He will continue to be with you until you reach your heavenly home. God is eternal. So openly embrace His presence and power, and "you will have a peace than transcends all understanding." I have had that peace, and it is indeed as sweet as honey. I pray God will strengthen me so I remain faithful and hopeful and enjoy His peace throughout the rest of my life.

Most of the incidents and encounters recorded here might have gone unnoticed by some, or even been taken for granted by others, but for a Christ follower like me—one who cries out daily for God's help—His presence and love comes alive ... especially in the trials of life.

I see it!

I feel it!

I experienced it!

There is a God, I have no doubt. And neither should you. He is all around you: just look into the faces of His angels that surround you.

TO GOD BE THE GLORY!

AMEN.

RESOURCES

Blackaby, Henry T. Blackaby Ministries International, Jonesboro, CA. www.blackaby.org

Chambers, Oswald. *My Utmost for His Highest*. Dodd Mead & Co., 1935; Grand Rapids: Discovery House, 1963. www.myutmost.org

Cherry, Reginald B. *God's Pathway to Healing Prostate*. Tulsa: Albury Publications, 2000. www.thepathwaytohealing.com; www.drcherry.com

Joncas, Michael. "On Eagle's Wings," copyright 1979. www.musicnotes.com; www.myspace.com; jmjoncas@stthomas.edu

LeTourneau, R. G. *Mover of Men and Mountains*. Chicago: Moody Press, 1967.

Mistra, Theodore. *The Shepherd and His Staff: A Guide to the Biblical Principles and Practices of Leadership*. Burlington: Castle Quay Books, 2017.

Nouwen, Henri J. M. *The Return of the Prodigal Son*. New York: Image Books/Doubleday, 1994. www.henrinouwen.org

Stanley, Charles. In Touch Ministries, First Baptist Church, Atlanta. www.intouch.org

Walsh, Patrick, and Janet Farrar Worthington. *Surviving Prostate Cancer*. Lake Forest: Wellness Central, 2007.
John Hopkins University website: http://urology.jhu.edu/patrickwalsh.

Warren, Rick. *The Purpose Driven Life*. Grand Rapids: Zondervan Publishing, 2002. www.purposedrivenlife.com; www.rickwarren.com

Wilkerson, David. Times Square Church, New York. www.tscnyc.org

OTHER TITLES BY CASTLE QUAY BOOKS

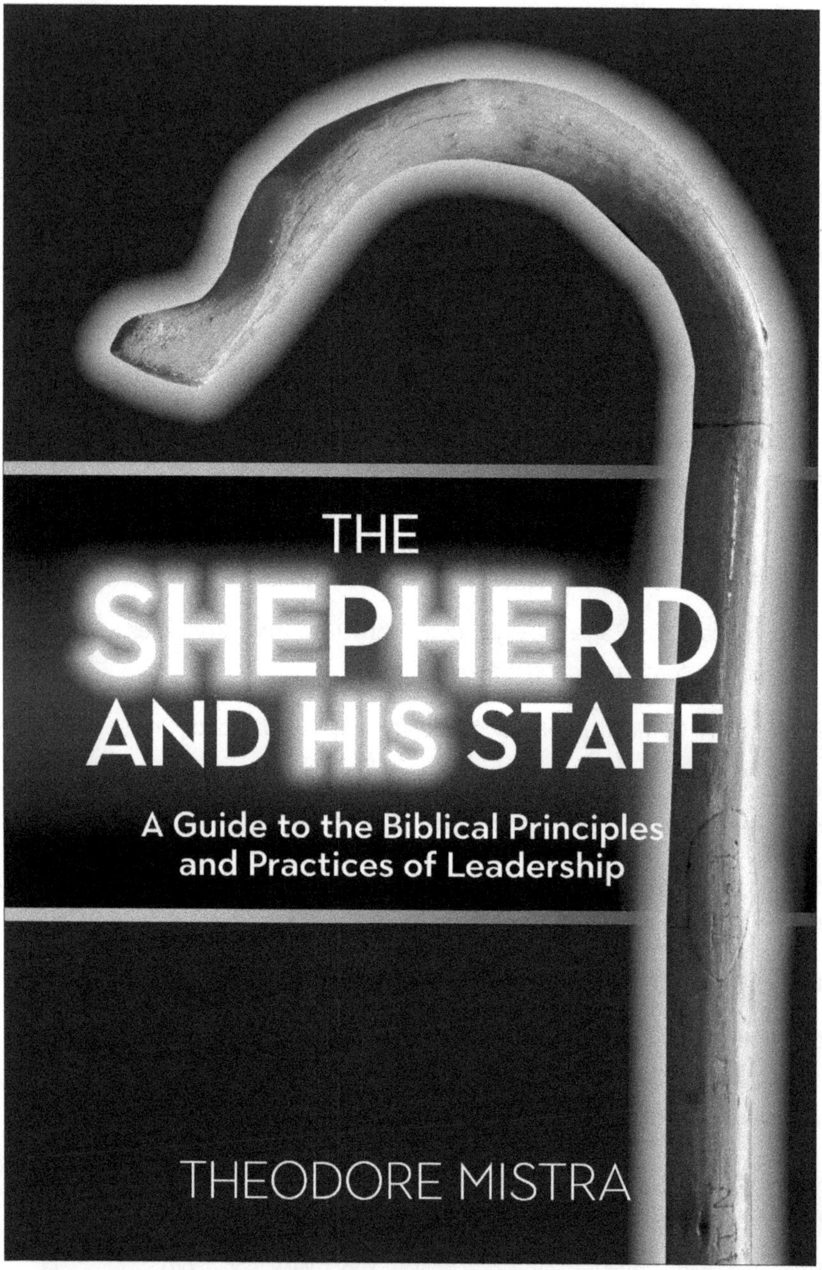

THE SHEPHERD AND HIS STAFF

A Guide to the Biblical Principles and Practices of Leadership

THEODORE MISTRA

OTHER TITLES BY CASTLE QUAY BOOKS

UNDER HIS WINGS

How Faith Conquers Fear

THEODORE MISTRA
AUTHOR OF *SURROUNDED BY ANGELS*

CASTLE QUAY BOOKS

OTHER TITLES BY CASTLE QUAY BOOKS

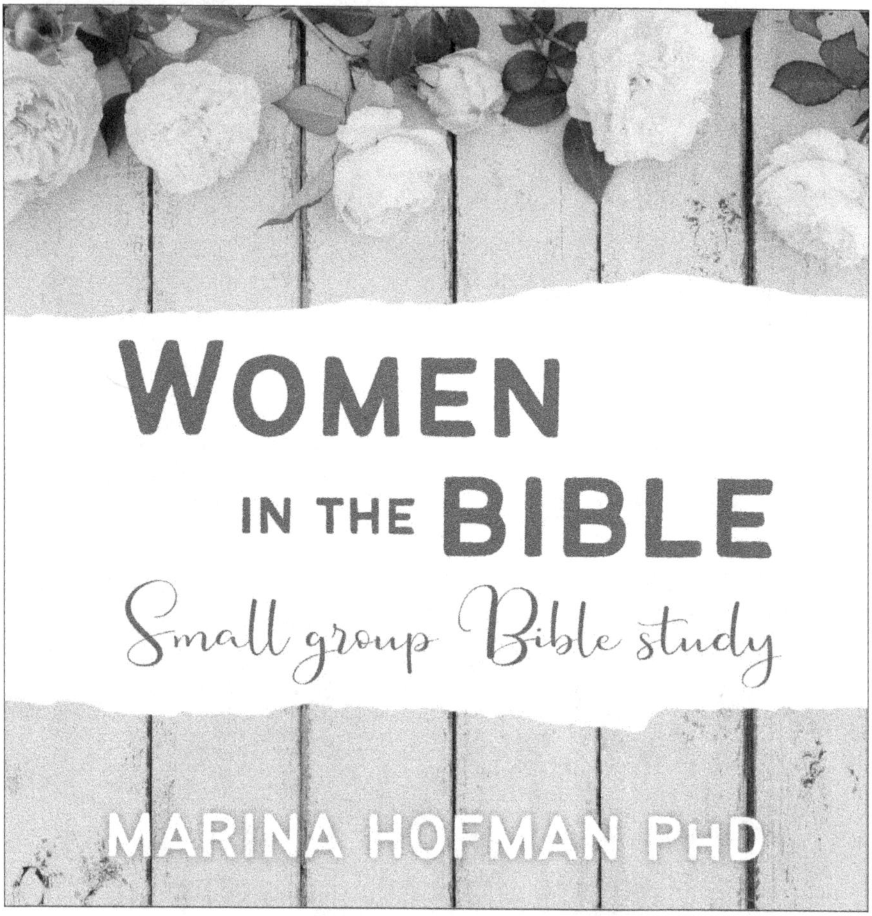

WOMEN IN THE BIBLE
Small group Bible study
MARINA HOFMAN PHD

OTHER TITLES BY CASTLE QUAY BOOKS

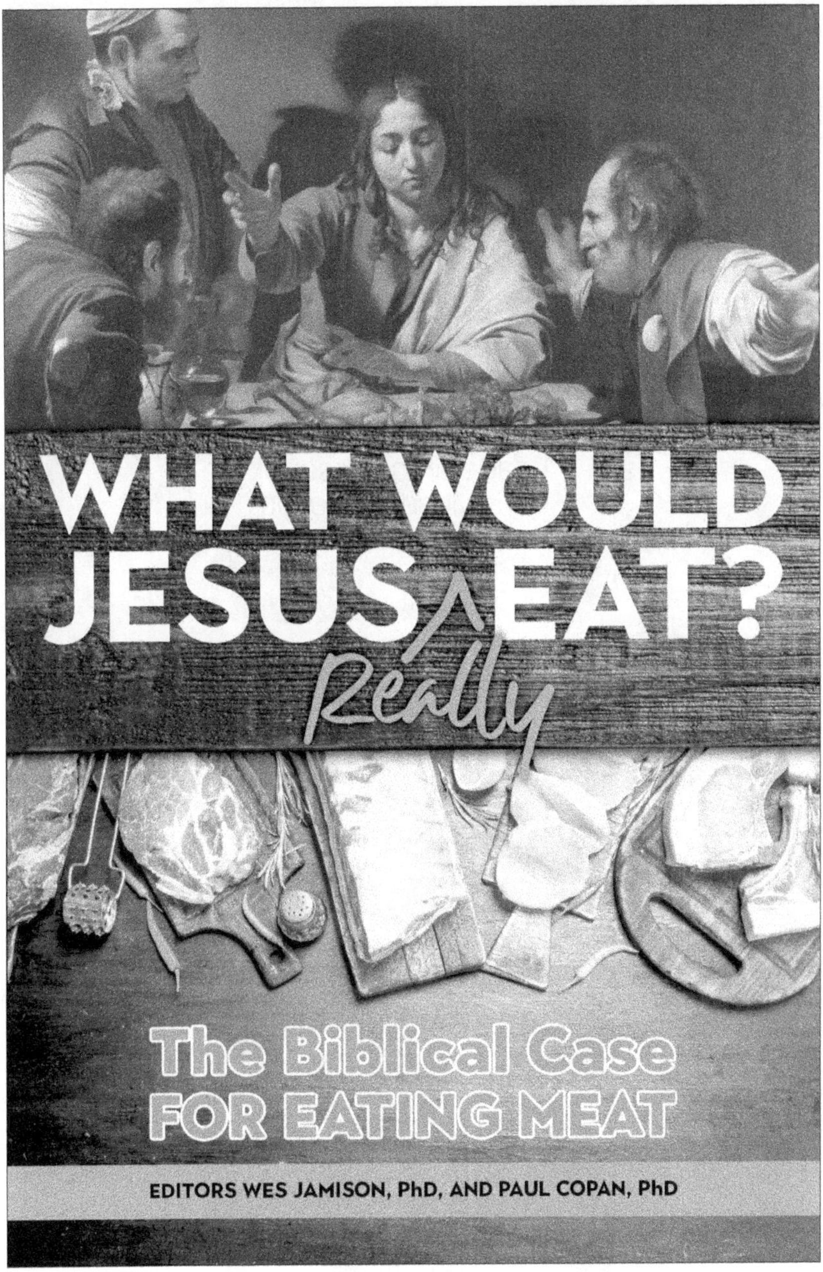

WHAT WOULD JESUS ⋀ EAT?
Really

The Biblical Case FOR EATING MEAT

EDITORS WES JAMISON, PhD, AND PAUL COPAN, PhD

OTHER TITLES BY CASTLE QUAY BOOKS

www.ingramcontent.com/pod-product-compliance
Lightning Source LLC
Chambersburg PA
CBHW072200100426
42738CB00011BA/2482